Britain and the Fa

Making Contemporary Britain

General Editor: Anthony Seldon
Consultant Editor: Peter Hennessy

Published

Northern Ireland since 1968
Paul Arthur and Keith Jeffery

Britain and the Falklands War
Lawrence Freedman

Forthcoming

British General Elections since 1945
David Butler

Suez
David Carlton

British Defence Policy since 1945
Michael Dockrill

Crime and Policing since 1945
Terence Morris

Institute of Contemporary British History
34 Tavistock Square, London WC1H 9EZ

Britain and the Falklands War

Lawrence Freedman

Basil Blackwell

Copyright © Lawrence Freedman 1988

First published 1988

Basil Blackwell Ltd
108 Cowley Road, Oxford, OX4 1JF, UK

Basil Blackwell Inc.
432 Park Avenue South, Suite 1503
New York, NY 10016, USA

British Library Cataloguing in Publication Data

Freedman, Lawrence
  Britain and the Falklands War. –
  (Making contemporary Britain).
  1. Falkland Island War, 1982
  I. Title   II. Series
  997'.11   F3031.5
  ISBN 0-631-16142-2
  ISBN 0-631-16088-4 Pbk

Library of Congress Cataloging in Publication Data

Freedman, Lawrence.
  Britain and the Falklands War / Lawrence Freedman.
    p.   cm. – (Making contemporary Britain)
  Bibliography: p.
  ISBN 0-631-16142-2: $30.00 (U.S.). ISBN 0-631-16088-4 (pbk.): $10.00 (U.S.)
  1. Falkland Islands War, 1982.   2. Great Britain – Politics and government – 1979–   I. Title.   II. Series.
  F3031.5.F74 1988
  997'.11–dc19   87-34114
                                                              CIP

Typeset in 11 on 13pt Ehrhardt
by Joshua Associates Ltd, Oxford
Printed in Great Britain by Page Bros (Norwich) Ltd

Contents

In memory of my father

General Editor's Preface

The Institute of Contemporary British History's series *Making Contemporary Britain* is aimed directly at undergraduates, sixth-formers and others interested in learning more about topics in postwar British history. In the series, authors are not attempting to break new ground but to present clear and balanced overviews of the state of knowledge on each of the topics.

The ICBH was founded in October 1986 with the objective of promoting the study at every level of British history since 1945. To that end it publishes books and a quarterly journal, *Contemporary Record*; it organizes seminars and conferences for sixth formers, undergraduates, researchers and teachers of postwar history; and it runs a number of research programmes and other activities.

A core theme in the ICBH's work is that postwar history is too often neglected in schools, institutes of higher education and beyond. The ICBH acknowledges the validity of the arguments against the study of recent history, notably the problems of bias, of overly subjective teaching and writing, and the difficulties of perspective. But it believes that the values of studying postwar history outweigh the drawbacks, and that the health and future of a liberal democracy require that its citizens know more about the most recent past of their country than the limited knowledge possessed by British citizens, young and old, today. Indeed, the ICBH believes that the dangers of political indoctrination are higher where the young are *not* informed of the recent past.

In this book Lawrence Freedman, one of the country's leading authorities on military matters, discusses the Falklands War. His clear approach analyses the issues that lay behind the conflict, the attempts to avert it, the principal events and the consequences of it for Britain and the international community.

Other merits of the book for students and general reader lie in the author's analysis of the merits (or otherwise) of the Government's action during the conflict.

The Falklands War did much to boost the morale of the Government and Britain's standing in the world. The book therefore can be usefully read alongside that in the series by David Carlton on Suez, which twenty-five years earlier damaged so badly the position of a previous Conservative government.

Anthony Seldon

Preface

From April to June 1982 British political life was dominated by a conflict over islands 8,000 miles away in the South Atlantic which had been seized by Argentina in pursuit of its claim of sovereignty and against the expressed wishes of the islands' 1,800 inhabitants who wished to remain British. This curious dispute, a legacy of the competitive colonialism of the eighteenth and early nineteenth centuries and the subject of spasmodic diplomatic exchanges ever since, suddenly erupted into a major clash of arms.

In many ways the Falklands War was wholly irrelevant to Britain's long-term problems, an atavistic if also enthralling distraction from the country's economic woes. But war offers a much more striking (if not necessarily a better) test of political leadership than economic policy or the day to day management of a complex society. The fate of the country was not at stake in the Falklands, but the fate of the Government was. Simply because these events were unique they revealed aspects of political life that are rarely prominent but are relevant to any overall assessment of the British political system. Lastly, in addition to its important role in any attempt to understand Britain's recent history or the character of its political life, the episode itself was intrinsically interesting and requires explanation.

The aim of this book is to provide the reader with a general background to the conflict and an insight into the sort of influences that shaped British policy-making. A much more detailed account of the interaction between Argentine and

British policy-making at this time is to form the subject of another work. The focus of this short book is much more parochial: to indicate the most important features of the crisis as they appeared at the time to the responsible British military and political leaders, and to put the crisis in its political context.

The conflict is widely held to represent a turning point in the fortunes of Margaret Thatcher's Conservative Government. The episode began with a major foreign policy humiliation for the Government, but was then turned into a major triumph. Before the full implications of the humiliation had had an opportunity to sink in, the Government had upped the stakes dramatically. Embarking on a major military expedition to re-take a remote set of islands situated some 8,000 miles away was a considerable gamble. It required not only the successful management of military operations and high-level diplomacy, but also the development and sustenance of a domestic political consensus. It was by no means inevitable that any of these requirements would be met. Much of this book is therefore concerned with suggesting reasons why they were met. Was the Government's success the result of good luck or good management? This involves asking more 'what if?' questions than is perhaps proper in a work of history. However, unless we examine carefully the peculiar conditions which made possible victory in this instance, erroneous conclusions might be drawn with regard to the management of similar crises in the future.

Such was the interest in the Falklands War at the time that it was the subject of a continual and intensive commentary. Once it was over the conflict was described and re-described from a variety of vantage points in a great number of books and articles. A considerable amount of further information has become available in the intervening years which qualifies but by no means discredits some of the early accounts. It is now possible to refine some of the early interpretations in the light of new evidence.

Although the events of those months are recent enough to stimulate for many some vivid images and arouse strong feelings ranging from anger to pride, they are also sufficiently distant to make it possible to begin to acquire a degree of historical perspective. Such a perspective allows us to question some of the myths that inevitably soon develop in the aftermath of a major military operation and are nurtured in subsequent political controversy.

The British Isles were not at risk during the conflict; nor were supplies of critical raw materials threatened. At stake were the intangibles of national pride and international norms, and if they were satisfied in the end, it is hard to say whether this was worth the cost in the tangibles of human and material resources. We will look at this question of the rights and wrongs of the confrontation in the discussions of the origins of the dispute over sovereignty with Argentina and its development until 1982 (chapter 2), of the management of the South Georgia incident which triggered the Argentine invasion (chapter 3) and in the concluding examination of whether the British military response was warranted (chapter 9).

A substantial majority of the British people was convinced from the start that some response was warranted after the Argentine occupation of the islands and came to accept the measures that the Government adopted to bring the war to a decisive conclusion. The success of the campaign overshadowed the preceding failure in crisis management and gave the war much of its long-term significance in boosting the popularity of Mrs Thatcher's Government and creating a reputation for resolve that the Prime Minister was happy to encourage. It may well be the case that the Conservative Party would have been returned with a substantial majority in the June 1983 general election despite the Falklands War. This question is addressed in chapter 8 as part of an examination of the performance of the political system at a time of limited war and in chapter seven which considers the role of public opinion in some detail.

The book concentrates on the political management of the conflict and the broad strategic factors that influenced its conduct rather than the detail of the military campaigns, on which there is now an ample literature. Because in limited wars such as this individual military engagements can have substantial political repercussions, a few such engagements – such as the sinking of the Argentine cruiser the *General Belgrano* – are examined fully. A brief assessment of some of the wider implications of the conflict for defence and diplomacy is provided in chapter 6.

My main objective is to provide a straightforward account of the origins of the war, the processes by which it came to a head in the early months of 1982 and was then resolved, at least temporarily, by force of arms. I hope to give a reasonably rounded analysis of this curious episode in contemporary British history, one that will not only help to remind us of and to understand its most critical moments, but will also stimulate discussion of some of the important issues it raised.

This book reflects the outcomes of many conversations on the Falklands War with both participants and observers. I am grateful to all of those who have shared their experiences and their ideas with me. I am particularly grateful to Virginia Gamba and General Julian Thompson for their valuable comments on the manuscript, and to Jean Murphy for typing the first draft. *Foreign Affairs* have also kindly agreed to allow me to reproduce material that first appeared in my article 'The War of the Falkland Islands, 1982' in the Fall 1982 issue of that journal.

1 Introduction

. . . Like two bald men fighting over a comb
Jorge Luís Borges

The War of the Falkland Islands began with a successful invasion of the islands by Argentine forces on 2 April 1982 and ended with their surrender to British forces ten weeks later. It was a textbook example of a limited war – limited in time, in location, in objectives and in means. Care was taken when it came to the treatment of civilians and prisoners and only in the later stages did non-combatants get caught in the fighting. The military casualties were severe – some 750 Argentine and 236 British dead – but this still represented only a small proportion of the forces committed.

In the character of the military operations, the clarity of the issues at stake and the unambiguous outcome, it was a curiously old-fashioned war. After 1945 the tradition of the short, sharp inter-state war was kept going by the Indians and Pakistanis and Arabs and Israelis. The major powers tended to get bogged down in more protracted 'anti-colonial' wars which were often wars of political complexity and strategic confusion. Such modern dramas were under way in the Middle East, South-West Asia and Central America in 1982. Many of these have yet to reach a conclusion. With the Falklands conflict we are now able to gain the advantage of a degree of historical perspective. This war came and went like something from the Victorian stage: a simple plot, a small but well-defined cast of characters, a story in three acts with a clear beginning, middle and end, and a straightforward conclusion which everybody could understand.

Britain has had its fair share of interventions in colonies and former colonies – Palestine, Malaya, Kenya, Cyprus, Aden – which have been handled with varying degrees of success and competence. The only year since 1945 when a British soldier has not been killed in action was 1968. Since then there has been a steady loss of men in Northern Ireland. The war in the Falklands was by no means the most costly in the lives of British servicemen – those in Korea, Kenya and Malaya all led to more than double the number of Falklands casualties, but these campaigns were spread out over years rather than months. Commitments of troops and equipment on the scale involved in the South Atlantic were made in the 1960s during the Borneo campaign but the build-up was neither so swift nor the use so intensive. The Korean War was an altogether more substantial affair, but Britain's role had been that of a supporting actor rather than a leading part. For the armed forces this was their first major test since 1945 of fighting on their own against an enemy as well equipped as themselves with modern military hardware.

A military challenge such as this cannot but be a critical test for the presiding political system. The conflict began as a major failure of that system. Its origins can be traced to a series of textbook mistakes by Britain in its own handling of the problem. These were combined with a degree of impetuosity on the Argentine side which created an element of surprise and made it relatively easy to occupy the islands – but at the cost of being in a poor position to hold on to them. Britain's eventual success in retrieving the islands was then held to reflect well on the political system.

Crises such as that in the Falklands arise when a relatively low-priority issue in one country has a high priority in another. A head of steam had been building up in Argentina over a number of years and had been clearly signalled in both diplomatic pronouncements and informal leaks in newspapers. The British Foreign Office was aware of the growing frustration in Buenos Aires but did not consider it to be approaching a danger point. Even as matters began to move to a head in early 1982 the foreign Office assumed that any direct action by Argentina would be gradual rather than decisive, putting pressure on Britain rather than presenting it with a *fait accompli*.

This assumption was not unreasonable and for much of this period may have been shared in Buenos Aires. However, the lack of attention in London to the implications of Argentine impatience and the lack of understanding of Argentine perceptions meant that it was difficult to appreciate the dynamics of the crisis once it picked up in earnest during March 1982.

The events in March had at their centre a group of scrap metal merchants who landed on the dependency of South Georgia without following the formal procedures. Argentina resisted the British attempts to ensure that these scrap metal merchants were all removed, thus raising the political temperature. The Argentine government, perhaps fearing that Britain was using this incident as a pretext to reinforce the Falklands, seized the opportunity to take the islands they called the Malvinas, which they accomplished on 2 April with only limited opposition from a small detachment of Royal Marines.

The next month was taken up by diplomatic activity to resolve the crisis, with American Secretary of State Alexander Haig attempting to mediate. Britain gradually stepped up the military pressure. A large task force was assembled with extraordinary speed and sent to the South Atlantic, using Ascension Island as a forward base. On 25 April, the South Georgia dependency was re-taken. This period ended on 29 April when Secretary of State Haig reported that his mission had failed to resolve the crisis; he blamed Argentina for the impasse and announced an American tilt in favour of Britain.

The next stage opened on 1 May with British air raids on the airfield at Stanley and some reactive Argentine attacks on the task force. The military results of all these engagements were limited. The most substantial military engagement took place the next day, however, when a British nuclear-powered submarine (SSN) sank the Argentine cruiser the *General Belgrano* with considerable loss of life. This was followed two days later by the sinking of the British destroyer *HMS Sheffield*. On 21 May the British landed on the islands at San Carlos and established a bridgehead in the face of substantial air attacks. A week later the settlements of Darwin and Goose Green were captured after some fierce fighting. British forces were then moved slowly across the island of East Falkland to the capital at

Stanley. In a series of engagements they overran Argentine defences on the periphery of Stanley; the Argentine garrisons on both the East and West islands surrendered on 14 June.

The political context

The sense of deep political failure with which the crisis opened had been transformed into a sense of resounding success by its close. As a result, the Falklands War can be seen as a watershed in post-war British political life. It was not quite the watershed it would have been if Britain had failed to respond to the Argentine seizure of the islands at the start of April 1982, or worse if Britain had attempted a military response and had then been defeated in battle. In either of these cases the episode would have been held to confirm Britain's post-war decline as a major power, would have raised questions with regard to other residual colonial or post-colonial commitments, such as Belize, and would have led to a painful reassessment of Britain's overall military effort. In domestic terms it could well have meant the end of the Conservative Government led by Margaret Thatcher after only three years in office, at a time when the economy was only just beginning to recover from a deep recession. Although the crisis was not manufactured to improve the Government's domestic standing, the short-term management of that crisis certainly helped revive its fortunes, although the impact of the episode on the Conservatives' re-election a year later remains a matter of psephological controversy.

As it was, the episode reinforced the status quo: it made it more difficult for Argentina to press its claim on the Falklands, more difficult to carry forward a review of Britain's defence policies and more difficult for dissidents within the Conservative Party, as well as the opposition parties, to dislodge Mrs Thatcher from No. 10 Downing Street.

Margaret Thatcher became Prime Minister in May 1979 when the Conservative Party was returned to office. She had wrested the leadership from Edward Heath after the two defeats of 1974. In contrast to the consensus politics increasingly practised by Heath in the early 1970s, she was more combative and radical in approach from the start. For those closer to the Heath model of Conservatism, who became known as the 'Wets' and who were strongly represented in her first cabinet, this radicalism appeared divisive and counter-productive. For much of the first two years of her administration the Prime Minister was consolidating her position within her own Government, sacking or displacing critics.

Mrs Thatcher's energies were concentrated on the economy, with inflation the main enemy in the short term and the major structural problems of entrenched trade union power and high levels of public spending the key challenges over the longer term. She came to power with inflationary pressures still strong in the economy, which the first budget of her Chancellor of the Exchequer, Sir Geoffrey Howe, aggravated rather than calmed by substantial increases in Valued Added Tax. A steep rise in oil prices resulting from the crisis over Iran added to inflation, but it also led to a strengthening of sterling in the international currency markets. With North Sea Oil Britain was now judged as an oil-producing as much as a manufacturing state and this encouraged the exchange rate to rise. Further encouragement was provided by high interest rates intended to dampen down the inflationary pressures. The combination of inflation and high exchange and interest rates increased the costs faced by British industry, left it very uncompetitive and so plunged the economy into recession and extremely high unemployment. Thus a year after the Conservatives took office, inflation and unemployment were both double what they had been in May 1979.

The result was a dramatic slide in the popularity of the Government and of the Prime Minister herself. The most natural beneficiaries would have been the Labour Party, but the party was still suffering from the splits which had plagued it through the 1970s and which now worsened. The election of left-winger Michael Foot as party leader, growing local influence by even more left-wing activists and a move towards unilateral nuclear disarmament, all put strain on party unity. Eventually in 1981 four leading members from the right of the party – Roy Jenkins, Shirley Williams, David Owen and

William Rodgers – left to form the Social Democratic Party. This soon began to work closely with the Liberal Party and provided the electoral phenomenon of 1981 with some dramatic by-election performances.

For the Government this was a testing time. As its popularity went down, unemployment reached 2.5 million, there were riots in Brixton and Toxteth, interest rates were rising again and there was dissension in the Conservative Party. Mrs Thatcher refused to be deflected and made few concessions to her critics. In a cabinet reshuffle of September 1981, leading 'Wets' Sir Ian Gilmour and Christopher Soames were ousted and Jim Prior was moved from Employment Secretary to Northern Ireland.

At the start of 1982 unemployment reached a plateau of three million at which it was to remain for more than five years thereafter. However, it is important to note that by this time the other economic indicators were beginning to look more hopeful. Interest rates – and the level of sterling – were starting to come down; consumer spending was starting to rise. The March 1982 budget was mildly expansionist. The Government was starting to recover in the opinion polls, with the Conservatives regaining ground lost to the Liberal–SDP Alliance during 1981. In a major by-election a week before the Argentine invasion of the Falklands, Roy Jenkins won the Hillhead Constituency of Glasgow for the SDP only with some difficulty.

Because Mrs Thatcher was preoccupied with the domestic economy, the main lead on foreign policy was taken by the Foreign and Commonwealth Secretary, Lord Carrington, a gifted diplomat in the traditional mould. The traditional diplomatic virtues – of tact, compromise, calculated ambiguity, focus on areas of agreement rather than disagreement – were not those most associated with Margaret Thatcher herself. However, in the first year of the Conservative Government these virtues demonstrated their worth in the skilful handling of the Rhodesian problem which was resolved successfully in 1980. Concern then shifted to the European Community, and what were seen to be excessive budgetary demands on Britain, and where the Prime Minister's tendencies towards a more direct approach came to the fore.

Mrs Thatcher's views on security matters whilst in opposition had tended towards the conservative orthodoxy of the time. She was deeply suspicious of the Soviet Union (by whom she was delighted to be labelled the 'Iron Maiden') and supportive of higher defence spending and nuclear deterrence. In line with American conservatives she inclined to the view that the Soviet threat was increasingly directed against the west's flanks in the Third World. In Government, Mrs Thatcher appeared to hanker after a renewed British involvement in military activities outside the NATO area. Some space was devoted in the Government's first Defence Estimates to a consideration of the need for a greater intervention capability. In February 1981, the Prime Minister even appeared to promise substantial involvement in the Rapid Deployment Force (RDF) planned in the United States.

This suggested a reversal of one of the most pronounced trends in British security policy over the previous two decades. Since the 1956 debacle at Suez British governments had shown great reluctance to get involved in large-scale military adventures overseas. Those operations that were undertaken tended to be of a counter-insurgency nature and linked to colonies or former colonies struggling to maintain political stability. In the 1960s the Government of Harold Wilson decided that Britain could no longer sustain a military presence 'East of Suez' and began to adjust defence policy to focus on security problems within Europe. In a passage in the 1966 Defence White Paper, somewhat ironic in the light of the Falklands, it was stated that Britain could no longer be expected to land or withdraw troops 'against sophisticated opposition outside the range of land-based air cover . . . unaided by our allies'.

The reluctance to resolve disputes through the use of armed force was underlined when Wilson ruled out the military option as a means of dealing with the Unilateral Declaration of Independence by the white minority government of Rhodesia in 1965. In 1974, with Wilson back as Prime Minister, Britain declined to use force when the military dictatorship in Greece sponsored a coup against the legitimate government in Cyprus. Britain had the right to intervene under the 1960 Treaty of Guarantee, to which it was a co-signatory, as well as forces on the Islands. Timely intervention could have helped avert a major crisis. However, intervention would have been a gamble because of the limited number of forces available and the difficulty of reinforcing them. If the immediate gesture of intervention had failed to produce the desired political result then there would have been a risk of British servicemen and civilians on the island becoming embroiled in a messy and protracted conflict. (In passing it might be noted that although British defence policy is geared to a challenge from a Communist state, the main occasions in recent decades when substantial applications of military power have been considered have resulted from right-wing challenges.)

The Conservative Government's willingness to base troops in Rhodesia during the transition to the independent state of Zimbabwe indicated an increased readiness to employ limited military power overseas. However, any inclinations to reorient defence policy away from Europe soon subsided as the costs and practical difficulties became apparent. In fact, the established tendency was decisively reinforced during 1981. The 1981 Statement on the Defence Estimates explained that the Government was considering only 'modest use of force to protect the interests of friendly local states and the West in strategic regions'. Resource constraints and the primary responsibility to NATO ruled out any idea of creating a substantial standing 'intervention force'. The modesty of what was likely to be available was underlined later that year – in June – with the publication of *The Way Forward*, which contained the results of a major defence review.

The review had been made necessary by the powerful pressures building up on the defence budget. Under a NATO agreement which had been negotiated under the Labour Government and endorsed by the Conservatives, defence spending was scheduled to grow at a target rate of 3 per cent per annum. However, Treasury attempts to rein in defence along with other public spending, generous pay rises to the armed services and ambitious procurement plans soon began to make it clear that the growth in the budget would be insufficient. Francis Pym was replaced as Secretary of State for Defence by John Nott in part because the Prime Minister was concerned that the military budget was not in firm enough control. In his first months at the Ministry of Defence Nott set about trying to match resources to commitments. He gained agreement that the 3 per cent target would be met until 1985–6, but in return he cut back on planned capabilities. There was to be a reduction in the numbers of destroyers and frigates from about 60 to 42, and a reduction also in dockyard capacity. One divisional headquarters of the British Army of the Rhine (BAOR) was to be removed. Only the RAF escaped lightly while the Navy took 57 per cent of the cuts in planned expenditure. The strategic message was clear: the centre of gravity of Britain's security policy was to be the centre of Europe. The continental commitment appeared to be winning out over Britain's maritime traditions.

It was thought by many at the time that these cuts had been made necessary by the Trident nuclear weapon system, the missiles for which were to be purchased from the United States. Certainly the government's determination to replace the old Polaris system with the latest generation of submarine-launched ballistic missiles did push the strategic nuclear force into a prominent position in the budgetary projections. However, the profile of expenditure on Trident meant that it did not loom large in the short term and so its cancellation would not have made it possible to avoid the choices between conventional capabilities that were made in 1981. The last defence decisions made prior to the Falklands War were in March, when John Nott announced a decision to buy the more advanced D-5 version of Trident so boosting the cost from £5 billion to £7.5 billion.

By 1982 it had become apparent that the budgetary prognosis of the previous year had been unduly pessimistic. The extra room for manoeuvre made it possible to reprieve two amphibious landing ships, *HMS Fearless* and *HMS Intrepid*, which had been scheduled to be cut. These came to play a critical role in the Falklands campaign. There was, however, no reprieve for *HMS Endurance*, the ice-patrol ship which had been taken to symbolize Britain's commitment to the Falklands, and which had been one of the most notorious casualties of the June 1981 review. Nor, despite naval protests, was there any revision of the strategic thrust of the review: defence policy was to follow NATO orthodoxy by concentrating on land and air forces capable of blocking a conventional invasion of West Germany, backed up by a nuclear deterrent. Therefore, the most significant feature of the Falklands War was that it was fought well out of the NATO area and with the Royal Navy the lead service. It was precisely the war for which Britain was planning least.

The structure of decision-making

The main forum for decision-making in Britain is the cabinet. Detailed decision-making, however, is handled in cabinet committees, of which the relevant one in this instance is the Defence and Oversea Policy Committee. It is chaired by the Prime Minister, and includes the Secretary of State for Defence, the Foreign Secretary and the Chancellor of the Exchequer. The Chiefs of Staff attend as necessary.

In March 1982 the relevant ministers were (now Sir) John Nott, Lord Carrington and Sir Geoffrey Howe. The Chief of the Defence Staff was Admiral Sir Terence (now Lord) Lewin. The other Chiefs of Staff were Admiral Sir Henry Leach (First Sea Lord), Field Marshal Sir Edwin Bramall (Chief of the General Staff) and Marshal of the Royal Air Force Michael Beetham (Chief of Air Staff). The committee is serviced, as are other cabinet committees, by the Cabinet Secretariat. The Secretary to the cabinet at the time was Sir Robert Armstrong.

As a result of British humiliation at the beginning of the crisis, Lord Carrington resigned, as did the second minister in the Foreign Office, Sir Humphrey Atkins, and Richard Luce, who as Minister of State was responsible for the Falklands. The new team was Francis Pym as Foreign Secretary and Cranley Onslow as Minister of State. The senior civil servant in the Foreign Office also changed at the same time, although this had long been planned. Sir Anthony Acland thus became Head of the Diplomatic Service in April, taking over from Sir Michael Palliser, who was due for retirement. Sir Michael stayed on as an adviser to the war cabinet for the duration of the conflict.

The changeover also affected the performance of the intelligence community, for which Sir Anthony had been responsible. He had been chairing the Joint Intelligence Committee, which included representatives from the security and intelligence agencies, the Foreign Office, Ministry of Defence and Treasury. The JIC considered assessments prepared by a staff of seconded civil servants and military officers, located in the Cabinet Office. In the Ministry of Defence there was greater continuity in both the Secretary of State John Nott, who offered to resign after the Argentine invasion but was asked to stay on, and the Permanent Under-Secretary, Sir Frank Cooper.

As the Government re-organized itself after the first shock of the occupation, decision-making passed to an inner group which soon became known as the 'war cabinet'. The full cabinet did discuss policy on the Falklands occasionally, but in general it was considered too large and potentially leaky and so was informed rather than consulted on the progress of the conflict. However a senior cabinet minister is reported to have said: '[Mrs Thatcher] had to carry the Cabinet on every major decision . . . That task force would never have sailed without Cabinet approval. There is no question of that.'

The 'war cabinet' was composed of the Prime Minister; the Deputy Prime Minister and Home Secretary, William (now Lord) Whitelaw, the Foreign Secretary, the Defence Secretary and the Paymaster-General and Chairman of the Conservative Party, Cecil Parkinson. Although this was defined in Whitehall as a sub-committee of the Defence and Overseas Policy Committee, in fact two of its members were not on that committee. Whitelaw added weight as a key member of the Government and the Party. Parkinson lacked the weight: officially he was given responsibility for the public relations side of the venture, but in practice, as a close associate of the Prime Minister, he was there to strengthen her position. It is also of note that the Chancellor of the Exchequer, Sir Geoffrey Howe, was not a member, although he was a member of the larger committee. In crises such as this the financial and economic questions often loom large (one only has to think of

Suez). As we shall note later, however, in the Falklands conflict the economic factor was the 'dog that did not bark'.

A final factor was the weakness of the two 'functional' ministers – Nott and Pym. Nott had offered to resign when the crisis broke and had performed poorly in the dramatic Parliamentary debate of Saturday 3 April. He had been encouraged to stay on but had little enthusiasm for the conflict and left the office six months after its conclusion, bravely denying its relevance for the 'broad strategic thrust' of British defence policy. Francis Pym was new to the Foreign Office and to the details of the dispute. He was promoted because of his position in the Party rather than any close relationship with the Prime Minister, and his influence was correspondingly limited.

The military advice to the war cabinet was channelled through the Chief of the Defence Staff, with other Chiefs of Staff in attendance when necessary. The command structure was complex. The Commander of the Task Force (CTF 317) was Admiral Sir John Fieldhouse, based at Northwood in North-West London. His two deputies were Air Marshal Sir John Curtiss (air) and General Jeremy Moore (land). Reporting directly to him were five task group commanders: Admiral Sir John 'Sandy' Woodward of the carrier battle task group; Commodore Michael Clapp of the amphibious task group; Brigadier Julian Thompson of the Landing Force Task Group; Captain Brian Young of the South Georgia Task Group; and Admiral Peter Herbert of the Submarine Task Group. Herbert was also based at Northwood from where he could be in direct contact with the submarines using satellite communications, the other commanders were all in the South Atlantic.

Although in the South Atlantic Woodward was *primus inter pares* the line of command did not pass through him but went directly to Northwood, and he could not be expected to take control of, for example, the amphibious operations when he had so much on his hands looking after his carrier group. One of the criticisms of the command structure was that there was no more senior figure interposed between the Task Group commanders and Northwood and based in the theatre of operations. As it was the overall picture had to be put together at Northwood on the basis of information received from the individual Task Groups, while the Task Group Commanders were distracted by the need to respond to continual requests from Northwood.

On 20 May General Moore was made Commander Land Forces. However, after flying to Ascension from London he was then stuck on the liner *QE2*, which was employed as a troopship, and not in direct communication with any of the commanders in the theatre of operations. He was only able to take effective command on arrival on 30 May. He had under his command two brigades. Brigadier Thompson became commander of 3rd Commando Brigade, with Brigadier Tony Wilson commanding the 5th Infantry Brigade.

The centralized nature of the decision-making is normal in crises such as this, dictated by the need for speed and secrecy. Yet because so much is at stake the requirements of accountability are also more intense. A small group taking more upon itself can expect to take the full blame if things go wrong as well as credit when they go right. For those taking the decisions the problem is that the success of their endeavours depends on the interaction of their moves with those being taken by another group of decision-makers on the opposing side. All these features make crises abnormal in terms of political activity, but also makes them a demanding test of any political system.

2 The Issue

That little ice-cold bunch of land down there
President Ronald Reagan, 30 April 1982

If initially many people found it difficult to take the conflict seriously, this was perhaps because of the unprepossessing nature of the territory at its heart. Nations are expected to go to war over something more than a collection of islands in an inaccessible and inclement area of the South Atlantic.

The islands

The islands consist largely of hilly grassland and shrub, few trees and barely 60 miles of roads. There are two main islands – East and West Falkland – as well as more than 100 smaller islands in the main group. In addition there are also a number of dependencies including South Georgia and the South Sandwich Islands. The capital, Stanley, where a majority of the population lives, is on East Falkland. In 1982 there were 20 miles of surfaced roads, all in the Stanley area, and at no point further that about two and a half miles from the outskirts in any direction except towards the airport. There was a gravel path from Stanley to Bluff Cove. The economy was once based on whales and now centres on sheep. There have been rumours of exploitable resources, including oil, in the surrounding waters but, along with the rest of the islands' economic potential, exploitation has been rendered difficult by the persistent dispute over their future between the islands' closest neighbour, Argentina, and their owners, Great Britain.

The Falkland Islands' population of 1,849 in the 1980

census would be barely sufficient to warrant one representative at the lowest level of local government in Britain. In fact the Islands have their own constitution. The British government was responsible for the government and defence of the Islands and for external relations in respect of them. The line of authority passed from the Secretary of State for Foreign and Commonwealth Affairs through the Governor of the Islands. From February 1979 this was Mr (now Sir) Rex Hunt. He was the local commander-in-chief and had full reserve executive and legislative powers, but in practice he administered with the assistance of an Executive Council composed of two elected members, two members nominated by the Governor, the Chief Secretary and the Financial Secretary. The latter two were also *ex officio* members of the Legislative Council which in addition had six elected members. The 1980 census showed the population to be 95 per cent British. Some 75 per cent were Kelpers, the name given to those born in the islands. The population reached its peak in the early 1930s at just under 2,400. It declined steadily to 2,200 by the early 1960s and then somewhat faster, at a rate of about 100 a year, to reach the 1980 figure. The decline was not as evident in Stanley, with more than 1,000 inhabitants, as in the area outside the capital, known as 'The Camp'. Most worrisome for future prospects was that a disproportionate number of those leaving were young women – often as a result of getting to know members of the Royal Marines, a platoon of which was resident on the islands since the mid-1960s as a form of protection. For young people generally the cumulative impact of tied-cottages and absentee farm-owners, inadequate services and lack of opportunities, was hardly enticing. The continuing dispute over sovereignty with Argentina, and the equivocal attitude in London, added to the doubts over the future.

At the time of the crisis the local economy was dependent on the export of wool, as it had been for a number of decades. Of about 40 farm units, the bulk were owned by companies rather than those occupying and working the land. The Falkland Islands Company (FIC) owned about 43 per cent of the total farm land and was generally economically dominant. In the 1976 Shackleton Report on the Island's economic prospects, the role of the FIC had been questioned, with the suggestion that the local government ought to be in a better position to influence company policy. FIC was not only the main producer but it also provided essential shipping, banking, distribution and marketing services. Ownership of the FIC was with the Derbyshire-based Coalite Group. For Coalite, FIC represented less than 1 per cent of its pre-tax income. The profitability of FIC's farming interests was in decline, only compensated to some extent by the increased profitability of its banking and trading activities.

For all Falklands farmers profits were in decline. With the prospects for wool prices unexciting, the overall economic situation in the early 1980s was unhealthy. At constant 1980 prices, GDP fell by a quarter from 1974 to 1980, when it was just under £4 million. The decline in national income was less marked, at only 4 per cent in constant 1980 prices. This was in part because the decline in profitability meant that less income than previously was being transferred abroad. Up to the mid-1970s outflows from the islands in terms of company dividends and undistributed profits, from which the United Kingdom extracted a considerable tax revenue, exceeded the inflows of investment and aid.

The other factor helping to hold up national income was an increase in UK Government investment and in other income from abroad, with philately a substantial provider. A quarter of the total income of the Falkland Islands Government came from stamps in 1981–2 (£0.6 million out of £2.47 million). According to the update of Lord Shackleton's study of the islands' economic prospects, delivered to the British Government in September 1982: 'The improved Government revenue from abroad, mostly from philatelic income, has helped avert a potentially catastrophic trend in national income.'

Investment had been minimal. Traditionally a high percentage of profits had been distributed by the Falkland Islands Company and other companies in the form of dividends. A lack of investment opportunities, the uncertainties of the political situation and the interests of the absentee owners in a steady income all contributed to parsimonious investment policies to the point where existing assets were not being properly maintained.

While in terms of running the islands the Falkland Islands Government could meet expenditure from the income raised in the islands, any serious development depended on UK aid. This had been increased after Lord Shackleton's first report in 1976. In 1981 total UK aid was £1,058,000. However, the 1976 Report had also noted that:

in any major new developments of the Islands' economy, especially those relating to the exploitation of offshore resources, co-operation with Argentina ... should, if possible, be secured. The sovereignty issue overhangs our Report, as it does the Falklands, and the absence of a settlement could well inhibit the full development of the Islands. This does not, of course, diminish the fact apparent to any visitor to the Islands that the population is British and, as was forcefully impressed upon us whenever the subject was discussed, is firm in its desire to remain British.

Thus the dilemma for Britain. The economic viability of the colony was in doubt yet the most obvious remedy was to cooperate with a country which claimed the Islands for itself, against the expressed wishes of the local population.

The dispute

The sovereignty question is at the heart of the issue ... we are not in any doubt about our title to the Falkland Islands and never have been.

Thus said the Foreign Secretary Francis Pym in the House of Commons on 4 May 1982. The argument with Argentina over sovereignty can be traced back to the decades in the first half of the last century when Argentina itself was just being formed out of former Spanish colonies. To Argentina the islands were part of Spain's legacy; to Britain they were not Spain's to bequeath. The matter was decided at the time by Britain's superior ability to enforce its claim to the islands, but Argentina never forgave nor forgot. Thus to make sense of the dispute in the second half of the twentieth century we need to go back to the first half of the nineteenth century and even earlier. The argument is based on assertions with regard to the legal meaning of often hazy events that took placed in confused circumstances, were subject at the time to a variety of interpretations and must now be assessed with regard to the changes in international behaviour and attitudes in the succeeding years.

The islands may have been sighted by an English sailor at the end of the sixteenth century, by a Spaniard even earlier and almost certainly by a Dutchman in 1600. The first recorded landing was not until 1690, by the crew of the British ship *Welfare*, whose captain named the sound between the two main islands after Viscount Falkland who was then, appropriately enough given the islands' later history, Treasurer of the Royal Navy.

The alternative name for the islands was provided by French sailors from St Malo in Brittany who called the islands the Iles Malouines, which the Spanish later recast as the Islas Malvinas. It was France who decided to colonize the islands because of their strategic position on the route to the Pacific. A settlement was founded on East Falkland in 1764 but this annoyed Spain, who controlled the South American mainland. France formally transferred its claim to Spain in 1767 for an indemnity equivalent to £24,000.

Meanwhile, Britain had been mounting its own expedition and in 1765 established its own settlement on West Falkland, with no contact being made with the French and later Spanish settlement on East Falkland. When the Spanish had sorted out the French they turned their attention to Britain. In 1770 a substantial Spanish force operating from Buenos Aires expelled the British settlers. Now it was the turn of Britain to protest. Spain decided that the islands were not worth war with Britain and allowed a return to the status quo ante, while insisting that this concession was without prejudice to the question of sovereignty. The British made no such statement. So the position became one of a Spanish settlement on East Falkland and a British settlement on West Falkland.

The British settlement was only maintained until 1774, after which all that was left was a plaque stating that the land was owned by George III. (The plaque itself was removed by the

Spaniards and taken to Buenos Aires; it was re-taken during a British invasion of Buenos Aires in 1806 but where it went thereafter is not known.) The Spanish settlement was more continuous. In 1811, when Spanish rule in Latin America came to an end, Spain abandoned the Falklands. They were occupied by the Government of Buenos Aires for the United Provinces, the forerunner of Argentina, in 1816, settled in 1820 and sovereignty was officially claimed in 1829. Britain, which had never renounced its own claim, protested and at the start of 1833 expelled the Argentine presence. The islands were formally established as a crown colony in 1840, and then settled with British subjects shipped there for the purpose. Britain retained control until 2 April 1982.

This continued to rankle with Argentina, though it is relevant in international law that it did not maintain *constant* pressure on the matter. Argentina claims that Spain never renounced her rights over the islands and that Spain's territorial jurisdiction of the area, including the Malvinas, was passed on to the newly independent state of Argentina in 1816. Britain did not raise the issue when conferring recognition on Argentina in 1825 nor had it complained earlier when Argentina acted as if it owned the islands. There was no British presence between 1774 and 1829, while the periods during which Argentine raised no objection to British claims lasted only 20 and 30 years respectively. Thus the British occupation of 1833 was illegal and remains so.

Against this the British argue that the settlement on West Falkland between 1766 and 1774 was sufficiently well established for an assertion of sovereignty that was capable of surviving the subsequent 50 years of absence before re-occupation. Britain had never recognized the Spanish title to the Islands which, in any case, was nullified by the withdrawal of the Spanish settlement in 1811 and the general Spanish withdrawal from the area. The subsequent attempts by Argentina to establish a valid title were insufficient to override the long-established British claim.

Whatever the quality of the British position as of 1833, which is hardly unassailable, Britain claims it to be reinforced by almost 150 years of continual occupation, with only spasmodic Argentine objections to this state of affairs, and the fact that the islanders themselves are happy with the constitutional status quo. According to Argentina this is beside the point as the islanders are of British origin, and so their preference is unsurprising, and they were put there to frustrate the Argentine position. In more recent years the argument has been re-phrased in terms of the more contemporary slogans of anti-colonialism and self-determination.

Although Britain has never publicly acknowledged the strength of the Argentine case, in previous years this has been recognized in internal discussions. Dr Peter Beck of Kingston Polytechnic, in evidence to the House of Commons Foreign Affairs Committee in 1982, identified a number of examples of these self-doubts. In 1829 even the Duke of Wellington, the then Prime Minister commented after perusing the papers that: 'It is not at all clear that we have ever possessed the sovereignty of these islands.' In 1946 a Foreign Office memorandum observed that the British occupation of 1833 could be interpreted as an act of 'unjustifiable aggression'.

The best that can probably be said is that neither side has a particularly good case. Britain's position is stronger with regard to West rather than East Falkland. The claim for the whole of the islands is based on the fact that Britain settled the islands long ago, albeit in confusing circumstances, that for long periods Argentina appeared to have no objection and that the local population is adamant that it wishes to stay British. The doctrine of prescription, upon which the British claim rests, essentially allows for a right of ownership to emerge out of continual possession. It would be extremely dangerous for international order if such a doctrine were now allowed to determine sovereignty over disputed territories on a regular basis. On the other hand, international order would not benefit if challenges to long-established occupation of territories were regularly mounted on the basis of the dubious methods of acquisition in previous centuries. The Organization of African Unity, for example, has made it a rule that states must live within the boundaries with which they gained independence, however arbitary or foolish their determination in colonial times, because of the chaos that would result from a series of contradictory territorial claims.

Politically, the important factor has been the strength not of the claim to sovereignty but of the islanders' determination to remain British. It is almost certain that if the islands had been uninhabited in 1982 Britain would have made no attempt to hold on to them in the face of Argentine claims. Argentina has the advantage of geographical proximity and a strong national sentiment that the Malvinas were unjustly taken from them.

Before moving on to the question of the negotiations in recent years to resolve these disputes, two points need to be made with regard to associated sovereignty claims. The first concerns the dependencies of South Georgia and the South Sandwich Islands. The legal position of the dependencies is much more clear-cut, as they were discovered by Captain Cook in 1775 and were never claimed by Spain. British sovereignty has been duly registered. The first letters patent were in 1908, when Britain described its sovereignty in the South Atlantic area. The large box of territory involved included the Falklands and Patagonia (Chilean and Argentine) as well as South Georgia, the South Sandwich Islands and the area which later became the British Antarctic Territory. (In 1917 this area was redefined in a new letter patent, which excluded the Falklands and Patagonia. It was acknowledged that to introduce the Falklands into this area was by implication to cast doubt on the validity of the earlier claim, while claiming Chilean and Argentine Patagonia might be considered a trifle provocative.)

On these islands there was a continuous British presence, before Argentina began to develop its claim to South Georgia (1927) and the South Sandwich Islands (1948), claim's based on geographic proximity. The dependencies are administered from Stanley. It was agreed by Britain in setting the terms for negotiations in the late 1970s that the sovereignty of the dependencies in practice needed to be discussed alongside that of the Falklands themselves.

In 1962 another set of territories which had been part of the dependencies (the South Orkney Islands, South Shetland Islands, Graham Island, Palmer Land and Coats Land) were detached to form the British Antarctic Territory. These have a similar pedigree to the remaining dependencies, with long-established British sovereignty based on first discovery being challenged later by Argentina and also, to a lesser extent, by Chile. The British Antarctic Territory is covered by the 1959 Antarctic Treaty which freezes competing claims over Antarctic territory and preserves the status quo for as long as the Treaty remains in force. It also demilitarizes the Antarctic. Under the terms of the Treaty any of the contracting parties can seek a review of the operations of the Treaty in 1991. The British Antarctic Survey, based at South Georgia, has served to establish Britain's continuing interest in its Antarctic territories. Although the interest of successive governments in the Antartic has not been high, it has been suggested frequently that its potential mineral wealth could become an important factor in determining long-term policies towards the region.

The negotiations

In the more recent period the islands only became a major source of tension between Britain and Argentina in the mid-1960s, when some private exploits by Argentine civilians reflected national feeling. The most notable of these was Operation Condor in September 1966, when an armed group of 20 young Argentines hijacked an Argentine Airlines DC-4 and forced it to land on the race course at Stanley. As a result of a similar but less dramatic incident in 1964 a platoon of Royal Marines (32 men) had been based in the islands, but this was subsequently reduced to an even more token force of one officer and five men. After the Condor incident it was restored to platoon strength at which it stayed for the next 15 years. It should be noted that the origins of the Royal Marine detachment lie with exploits of this sort (with which a small armed unit could be expected to deal direct) rather than any attempt to deter an invasion by Argentine forces.

The official Argentine approach at this time was to raise the issue in the committee of the United Nations dealing with colonialism. In December 1965 General Assembly Resolution 2065 was passed which accepted the Argentine view that the

British position in the Falklands represented a form of colonialism and urged the two countries to negotiate a solution 'bearing in mind ... the interests of the population of the Falkland Islands (Malvinas)'. Britain abstained in the vote.

The Labour Government in Britain rejected the claim that its position was illegal but was prepared to discuss the issue. The Government had concluded that in practical terms its position on the islands was not strong. In March 1967 it indicated to Argentina that it would be prepared to cede sovereignty under certain conditions, provided that the wishes of the islanders were respected. The Government thus conceded that there was a case to answer.

To the Foreign Office, British interests with Latin America as a whole ranked higher than those of a couple of thousand islanders. Nevertheless, the question of the role of the local population dogged the negotiations from the start. As with practically all the residue of its Empire, Britain has found itself holding on to colonies against its better judgement because of the strong preference of the colonized for British rule as against the most likely alternatives. The islanders have always shown a marked antipathy to Argentina.

When the attitude of the British Government became known to the islanders in 1967 there began what became a familiar pattern of open contacts with British MPs and newspapers, who then made such a fuss that the responsible ministers were obliged to promise that nothing would be done against the wishes of the islanders. It was as part of an effort to channel these protests that the Falkland Islands Emergency Committee was established. It was set up in the course of a visit to Britain by four members of the islands' Executive Council in 1968. When it was re-formed in 1973 as the UK Falkland Islands Committee it adopted as its objectives: 'To assist the people of the Falkland Islands to decide their own future for themselves without being subject to pressure direct or indirect from any quarter.' Its members were drawn from all political parties, maintained good links with the press and kept alert for any sign of a weakening of the British Government in the face of Argentine pressure.

Despite the protests the Foreign Office agreed a Memorandum of Understanding with Argentina in August 1968 which raised the possibility of a 'final settlement' which would 'recognize Argentina's sovereignty over the islands from a date to be agreed'. This required agreement on securing the interests of the islanders through safeguards and guarantees. Britain promised that no transfer of sovereignty would take place if it was unacceptable to the local population.

The efforts of the then Minister of State Lord Chalfont to explain this policy met with a hostile reception. With it now becoming a domestic political necessity in Britain to reaffirm that there would be no transfer of sovereignty against the wishes of the islanders, and an equal domestic necessity in Argentina to reject such a condition, the Memorandum of Understanding failed to serve as the basis of an agreement. The cabinet decided to keep talking with Argentina so as to prevent a further deterioration in relations.

The Government's view was that the logic of the situation favoured Argentina. However, the stubbornness of the islanders, fortified by supporters in the House of Commons, made it impossible to concede the point of principle to Argentina. Yet Britain was not willing to devote resources to the islands because it could not share the population's hope of a long-term future under the British flag. The compromise solution was to attempt to show good faith in negotiations and yet push the islanders as gently as possible into cooperation with Argentina, for example by making them dependent on Argentina for communication with the outside world.

This was the approach that was adopted in the round of talks that began in 1969 and continued into the term of office of the Conservative Government of Edward Heath. In September 1971 an agreement was signed as a result of which air and sea links were established between the islands and the Argentine mainland, and other measures were taken to facilitate ease of movement between the two. However Argentina was not prepared to put aside the question of sovereignty for long and after this agreement was signed, sovereignty was put back on the agenda. Facing British resistance, it turned again to the United Nations which obliged with a further resolution in 1973 urging negotiations towards a settlement of the sovereignty issue.

The Heath Government began to explore alternative approaches, and in particular a condominium with Argentina. This idea was taken up by the Labour Government which returned to office after the March 1974 general election. Once again the islanders were less than enthusiastic; while prepared for talks, they did not want to participate themselves. The Government abandoned this idea.

Next the Government looked to a more indirect approach; joint Argentine-British development of the South-West Atlantic region. Argentina, however, was no longer interested in any talks that excluded sovereignty and so this idea faltered. Argentina in turn raised the idea of a transfer of sovereignty followed by a lease-back to a British administration for a number of years.

In the context of these various ideas, the Government commissioned the survey of the islands' long-term economic prospects from a team led by Lord Shackleton. The group reported in May 1976; I have already mentioned some of its findings. The inquiry, suggesting as it did a longer-term commitment by Britain to the development of the islands, led to protests from Argentina, with dire warnings of the consequences should Britain continue to fail to respond to Argentine concerns. An unsuccessful attempt by the Argentine Navy to arrest a research ship, the *RRS Shackleton*, in Falkland waters provided a reminder of the risk of violence.

At that time *HMS Endurance*, which had entered service in the South Atlantic in 1967 as an ice-patrol vessel, combined hydrographic work with the provision of a limited naval presence. In another of the familiar scenes from this saga, the Labour Government's Defence Review of 1974 had decided to phase out *HMS Endurance*. The furore over the Shackleton Report led to the ship's patrols being continued for a further period. Regular appeals from the Foreign Office persuaded the Ministry of Defence to continue with patrols – until the next Defence Review of 1981.

A more successful Argentine action in 1976 was to establish a small presence on South Thule, one of the South Sandwich

Islands. Though at first denied by Argentina, the incursion was discovered by *HMS Endurance*. Britain protested privately but did little. The incident did not become public knowledge until 1978.

The Labour Government was unwilling to raise expenditure on the islands in line with the recommendations of Lord Shackleton. Foreign Secretary Anthony Crosland observed pointedly: 'There are more urgent claims from much poorer communities. The right political circumstances do not exist.' He stressed those aspects of the Shackleton Report which noted the benefits that might flow from cooperation with Argentina, rather than those that demonstrated the potential for economic development without Argentine help. Ted Rowlands became the next in the line of junior Foreign Office ministers to travel to the islands and warn of the dangers of continued intransigence. As a concession he offered close involvement in negotiations with Argentina. The view within the Government was that the best outcome would probably be a lease-back with economic cooperation between the two countries. It was hoped that prolonged discussions would allow time for the merits of such an approach to be recognized in both Britain and the Falklands.

Initially the talks went reasonably well, but in late 1977 there were fears that Buenos Aires was losing patience with a diplomatic route, and might attempt more direct military action instead. This concern was reinforced by a spurt of military threats and complaints from Argentina, reflecting frustration with the lack of progress. In case there should be some limited aggression in the run-up for the second round of talks, scheduled for December, the Government authorized sending a nuclear submarine and two frigates to the area. The contingencies with which this force was designed to deal never materialized, however, and so it remained covert (and was never picked up by Argentine intelligence). The talks did produce a limited agreement in 1978 on scientific cooperation in the dependencies but even this was too much for the Falkland Islands Councillors, who effectively exercised a veto.

The Conservative Government that came to office in May

1979 was presented with the same set of options as its predecessors and came to the same conclusion. In 1980 the junior Foreign Office minister responsible for the Falklands, Nicholas Ridley, followed his predecessors in soon becoming convinced that the islands would decline into non-viability unless some settlement was reached with Argentina. The option he favoured was to transfer sovereignty of the islands to Argentina but then to lease them back. However, he was not supported in the relevant cabinet committee. This has been one of those issues where backbench sentiment exceeds ministerial interest, and Ridley was given no mandate to solve the issue by the lease-back method or to give anything away to Argentina.

Ridley visited the islands in November 1980. The islanders were now accustomed to these visits, which were treated with suspicion. One of the options Ridley offered for the future was freezing the status quo, which was obviously the local preference. Despite this, Ridley himself believed there was considerable readiness to examine the merits of lease-back, especially if the lease had a long enough time-span – at least 99 years. It has been suggested that a more tactful approach might have garnered more support. When the Falklands Islands Joint Council expressed its view in January 1981, it was to opt for continual negotiations with Argentina but only in order to agree to freeze the dispute over sovereignty for a specified period of time.

At any rate, on reporting back to the Commons on his return at the start of December Nicholas Ridley received an even more unfriendly reception. He noted that the dispute was causing 'continuing uncertainty, emigration and economic stagnation in the islands', he mentioned the alternatives – a freeze and lease-back – and suggested that their consideration would be shaped by the 'advice' and 'guidance' provided by the islanders. Although he did promise that any settlement would need to be endorsed by the islanders and Parliament, the fact that he did not simply say that the islanders' wishes would be paramount caused concern in the House. There were few voices raised in his support. The general view was that there was nothing on sovereignty worth talking to Argentina about, and that any hint that there might be was dangerous and unsettling to the islanders.

This was taken as a formidable demonstration of the power of the Falkland Islands lobby, which had become skilled in tapping a vein of sentimental attachment on both sides of the House of Commons. Politically this reinforced the Government in the view that upsetting this lobby would cause a major fuss, for little purpose.

The policy became one of continued negotiations with Argentina in the hope that the talking itself would contain Argentine frustration and bring Falkland opinion round. When, in talks in February 1981, Nicholas Ridley proposed the freeze option to Argentina it was rejected outright. The British intelligence community began to pick up signs of growing Argentine impatience over the lack of progress on sovereignty. Meanwhile the position of the islanders hardened as a result of the October 1981 elections to the Legislative Council. For the moment, however, the Argentine threat was not judged severe enough to warrant any further attempt to convince the islanders and their Parliamentary supporters of the need for concessions. But the room for manoeuvre was declining steadily. At the end of 1981 Lord Carrington hoped there might still be just enough to prevent new talks with Argentina ending in complete stalemate.

3 The Crisis

It was the Wednesday evening, when there was a message saying that their fleet had broken off for some exercises. It looked as if their fleet was going to Port Stanley. It looked as if they had armed equipment on board. All of a sudden I said — this is the worst week I am ever going to live through.
Prime Minister Margaret Thatcher; interview with George Gale, *Daily Express*, July 1982

... we conclude that we would not be justified in attaching any criticism or blame to the present Government for the Argentine Junta's decision to commit its act of unprovoked aggression in the invasion of the Falkland Islands on 2 April 1982.

Thus the concluding paragraph of the report of the Committee of Privy Counsellors, chaired by Lord Franks, which had been set up to 'review the way in which the responsibilities of Government in relation to the Falkland Islands and their dependencies were discharged in the period leading up to the Argentine invasion'. It reinforces the suggestion apparent in the words of the Prime Minister which open this chapter that the Argentine invasion came upon the British Government as an unprovoked bolt from the blue. As a result, the Franks Report was widely greeted with derision as something of a whitewash, and substantial evidence was found in the main body of the report to undermine the conclusion. Would a stronger conclusion have been warranted?

The committee was made up of members of the political elite who recognized that all decision-makers, as they attempt to make sense of complex events with imperfect information, are fallible. Better decisions might have been taken, but the ones that were taken were not unreasonable given all that was known at the time. The committee pointed out that the political and military constraints on the Government's position had been inherited and this left it with few options in its dealings with

Argentina. Moreover, Argentine decision-making moved quickly and in unexpected directions during March 1982. The decision to invade was not taken until late in the month. Different British responses to Argentine moves in the preceding weeks and months might have made a difference, but there is no certainty that they would. The committee's strictures were reserved for the intelligence community, which had been 'too passive in operation to respond quickly and critically to a rapidly changing situation which demanded urgent attention'.

This they saw as a defect in the Joint Intelligence machinery when 'working in an area of low priority'. This particular set of problems may, however, have been a symptom of the operation of the Government as a whole in an area of low priority. As we saw in the previous chapter, the roots of the problem go back a long way. The Government inherited an issue where the logic of the situation favoured Argentina but past commitments and domestic political opinion favoured the Falkland Islanders. The two positions had become increasingly polarized. The Government was aware of this but continued to hope that in the long term common sense would prevail and the two positions would be reconciled. The problem with this approach was that reconciliation was never likely to happen naturally; it would rather require an active effort by Whitehall to extract compromises, of which the first would have to be acceptance by the Islanders that some change in their constitutional status had to be considered. Lord Carrington rejected the option of an active campaign of public education to bring home the need for eventual compromise, on the grounds that there would be a political backlash if the Government was seen to be pressurizing the islanders. So long as Argentina was not actually putting pressure on Britain it was doubtful whether the moment would ever seem propitious to put pressure in turn on the Islanders. This approach was dependent on recognizing the moment at which the implementation of the campaign could no longer be delayed and the problem was that at such a moment a campaign of political education could not bring results sufficiently quickly to hold off the Argentine pressure.

A second and more serious consequence of the low priority

attacted to the problem was that policy was allowed to get dangerously out of kilter. The lack of political will in London to solve the dispute once and for all in some deal with Buenos Aires was combined with an unwillingness to accept full responsibility for the long-term security and prosperity of the islands.

Effectively, by failing to prepare the ground for either greater concessions by Britain in later talks or for a strengthening of Britain's negotiating hand by demonstrating a serious commitment to the islands, Britain had, in the words of the Franks Report, 'handed over the initiative' to Argentina. Putting off awkward decisions was politically the easiest course. Unfortunately, it required Argentine consent.

Without adequate forces in place, British defensive plans had depended on the dispatch of reinforcements by sea at the first sign of trouble. As it takes at least three weeks to cover the 8,000 miles from Britain, this required a generous warning time. Whenever the Falklands issue flared up Britain had to decide between taking strong military action while the crisis was still in its early stages, or alternatively, for the sake of quiet diplomacy, delaying preventive military measures until possibly too late. In 1977 the Labour Government's response to an invasion scare was to send some frigates and a nuclear submarine to the area, but the decision was rendered easier by the fact that the vessels were relatively close for quite unconnected reasons. It is doubtful that Argentina was then either considering invasion or aware that the British were taking action to forestall one.

The contradiction in the policy became acute in June 1981 when it was decided to scrap the ice-patrol ship *HMS Endurance* as part of the Defence Review. This ship, although sparsely armed, constituted the sole regular British naval presence in the South Atlantic and had taken on a symbolic importance far beyond its military capabilities. The Royal Navy had never attached a high priority to its preservation, offering it as a sacrifice when cuts were sought.

In 1981 the Ministry of Defence was determined to reduce naval capabilities even if this meant letting *HMS Endurance* go. The Foreign Office warned that this could well be misread in

Buenos Aires. It would leave only a small garrison of Royal Marines to deter Argentina from attempting to re-take the Falkland Islands by force. The islanders protested vigorously. The withdrawal would 'further weaken British sovereignty in this area in the eyes not only of the islanders but of the world'. The Government could not claim that it had not been warned that the decision on *HMS Endurance* was widely seen (including in Argentina) to reflect a less than total commitment to the long-term protection of the islands.

The Home Office joined with the Ministry of Defence in adding to the Foreign Office's problems by further undermining the appearance of British commitment. It failed to make special provision for the islanders in the British Nationality Act of 1981, which limited citizenship rights in British dependencies; thus many suffered a loss of 'Britishness'. Again, from the point when the Bill was first mooted in 1980, the Government had been warned of the interpretation that could be put on this measure.

Thus at a time when those most concerned with the issue were hardening their positions, the British Government was weakening its own. Britain now could offer neither compromise to Argentina nor a credible long-term commitment to the Falkland Islands. The only negotiating position left was prevarication.

British policy-makers were aware that feeling in Argentina was running high. They hoped a complete deterioration of relations could be avoided by continued negotiations. It was presumed that if there was a deterioration this would be marked by gradually escalating action starting from a low level with diplomatic and economic measures. The failure of the Ridley initiative left a policy vacuum. Although minutes were circulated and informal discussions took place, there was no formal discussion of Government policy towards Argentina and the Falklands outside of the Foreign Office from January 1981 to the day of the Argentine invasion on 2 April. The Latin America Current Intelligence group met 18 times between July 1981 and March 1982 but did not discuss the Falklands on any of those occasions. The situation in Belize had a higher priority.

The hope that the dispute could be prevented from turning critical was given a boost in February 1982 when new talks produced some agreement on negotiating procedures and were described in the joint communiqué to have been conducted in a 'cordial and positive spirit'. Unfortunately the feeling in Buenos Aires was quite different. From there a much more hard-line Argentine communique emerged which stated that the objective of the negotiations would be to 'achieve recognition of Argentine sovereignty', that time was short and failure to produce results would mean the negotiations might be terminated and another 'procedure which best accords with [Argentine] interests' be adopted.

In Buenos Aires patience with Britain had run out. The 15Oth anniversary of the British seizure of the islands, in January 1983, appeared as a sort of deadline. The Government of General Leopoldo Galtieri, which had come to power in December 1981, had the issue high on its agenda. It is now known that while the actual decision to invade the Falklands was not taken until 26 March (a few days earlier than assumed in the Franks Report), planning for a possible invasion had begun in January 1982. The Argentine Government noted precedents (such as the Indian takeover of the Portugese colony of Goa in 1961) where after initial condemnation the international community had learned to accept the results of decisive military action. In Washington, the Galtieri regime was judged to represent the acceptable face of military dictatorship. It was cooperating with the United States to support other right-wing regimes in Central America. The hope was that Washington would not be too cross if Las Malvinas were retrieved.

The British Government had shown itself averse to the use of force to solve these matters in the past, and in sorting out the Rhodesian problem Mrs Thatchers had demonstrated considerable pragmatism and prudence. On this particular issue, Britain had managed to convey the impression of intransigence in negotiations on the principle of sovereignty but no real interest in holding on to the islands.

The timing of the Argentine invasion indicates a lack of concern for minimizing Britain's ability to respond, and indeed

Argentine leaders have since confirmed that they assumed Britain would not respond. Much of the British fleet was home for Easter, which facilitated the rapid assembly of a task force. Two months later and the British position would have been more stretched, with a group of warships including the carrier *HMS Invincible* in the Indian Ocean, and even further away from the South Atlantic. *HMS Endurance* was on its last patrol. Any force which reached the South Atlantic would only have done so at the height of winter and after a long delay. Furthermore, Argentina was only just starting to take delivery of new arms, including the Exocet-carrying Super-Etendards from France. Within a few months, its own forces would have been much better equipped.

This indicates that the invasion had not been scheduled for the start of April months in advance but was the product of the events of March 1982. The British Government cannot therefore be blamed for failing early in 1982 to anticipate the timing of an invasion that had not yet been agreed in Argentina. The next charge the Government faces, however, is that it failed to manage the events of March 1982 to prevent this decision being taken.

The trigger: South Georgia

The trigger for the crisis was the curious incident of a group of scrap metal merchants, led by Snr Davidoff, who landed on the dependency of South Georgia on 19 March. Snr Davidoff had a contract to take materials from Leith but no means of doing so. The Argentine navy was happy to help him so as to be able to establish a presence which might continue once the British Antarctic Survey left in October. There was no need for this presence to be established surreptitiously. The arrangement had been agreed with the British Embassy in Buenos Aires. However, the naval ship taking the scrap metal men to the islands failed to follow the normal formalities, in particular by not paying a courtesy call on the British Antarctic Survey base at Grytviken.

If there had not been a developing tension in Anglo-

Argentine relations at this point, this incident might have passed off with a mild official protest by Britain. Such was the instinct of the British Embassy in Buenos Aires. However, others were more suspicious. In 1977 Argentina had established a presence in an even more remote dependency – South Thule – and there was concern that the plan was now to do likewise on South Georgia. The Governor-General of the Falklands, Rex (now Sir Rex) Hunt, fortified by reports from the captain of *HMS Endurance*, warned that these scrap metal merchants were instruments of the Argentine Junta. Any instinctive desire on the part of the Foreign Office to sort the matter out through private diplomacy was undermined by the news of the 'landing', and the accompanying raising of the Argentine flag, leaking in the British press. This led to demands in Parliament for a reassuring statement. On 21 March the Foreign Office was still attempting to play the issue down; two days later, with the issue now aired in Parliament and the media, it was obliged to take a firmer line.

In attempting on 23 March to reassure both Parliament and the Falkland Islanders, Richard Luce (Nicholas Ridley's successor in this Foreign Office post) alarmed the Argentines. First, the despatch of *HMS Endurance* to South Georgia, apparently to expel the scrap metal merchants, brought national honour into play. Argentine warships were sent to warn that such an expulsion could escalate. Then an attack on the Argentine Air Force airline (LADE) office in Stanley on the night of 20–21 March, which had seen a Union Jack placed over the Argentine flag and 'tit for tat, you buggers' written in toothpaste on a desk, did not help. Secondly, hints that a nuclear submarine and even frigates were being sent by Britain to the South Atlantic led to some concern that the particular incident on South Georgia was being used as a pretext to reinforce Britains military position in the area. If true this would complicate and perhaps rule out any future plans, which were still being drawn up, to take the islands by force. On 26 March therefore the Junta decided to strike while the opportunity presented itself.

All the contradictions of Britain's Falklands policy were being pushed to the fore. The Government insisted that it could not acquiesce in any 'infringement of British sovereignty', yet there was very little it could do to back its position by force. There would always have had to be good reason to send forces specially to the South Atlantic. It would involve taking ships away for a long period from other duties and high expenditure on fuel. Even maintaining two ships in the squadron watching over the Gulf of Oman since 1980 had made a large dent in the Navy's fuel allocation. Even if it had been decided at the first sign of trouble to send a task force it would have taken weeks for it to arrive.

Although there were signs from the start of the year that at least some elements in Argentina were considering a military solution to the Falklands issue, there was no expectation that this would lead to anything dramatic in the immediate future. It was expected that any escalation wopuld be more gradual. Indicators of an intent to invade, such as speculation in the Argentine press, were not judged to be significant in themselves: such indicators had appeared too often before. Warnings from the captain of *HMS Endurance* about a change in the Argentine attitude noticed on his visits to Argentine ports, and from the Governor-General of the Falkland Islands, were suspected to reflect special pleading.

In March 1982 there was therefore a disposition in Whitehall, and in the British Embassy in Buenos Aires, not to react strongly to the incident on South Georgia. It was reinforced by a desire not to upset by provocation the good work that had gone into improving relations with Latin America, including Argentina, over the previous few years as well as a belief that the problem could be solved through diplomatic channels. The Prime Minister observed to the Commons on 3 April,

had I come to the House at that time and said that we had a problem on South Georgia with ten people who had landed with a contract to remove a whaling station, and I had gone on to say that we should send HMS "Invincible", I should have been accused of war mongering and sabre rattling.

With its Navy at sea and only two days away from the islands, the temptation for the Argentine Government to take the historic step at the end of March 1982 seemed irresistible. When the invading forces arrived on 2 April, the British Marines were in no position to resist and soon surrendered. Resistance on South Georgia was no more successful, if a little more spirited, and Argentine forces took some casualties. Nowhere were there casualties among the British forces or the civilians, a fact which the Argentine Government appeared to believe would make the invasion tolerable. In Britain the news was received with disbelief. The sense of Government impotence and incompetence was reinforced by the confusing statements made to Parliament by Carrington's number two, Sir Humphrey Atkins, on the position in Stanley.

The Government's misjudgement was in not recognizing the change in political conditions in Buenos Aires, the seriousness of this crisis compared to its predecessors, and the influence of its own moves and statements during the South Georgia incident on Argentine perceptions. Ministers in Britain had their minds on other things: the Foreign Secretary's visit to Israel and another row over the European Communities' budget. As late as 29 March, in the course of a Parliamentary debate about the Trident programme, the Defence Secretary had appeared to dismiss the problem. When asked by Keith Speed, who had resigned as Minister for the Navy just before John Nott had prepared his 1981 Defence Review, how the country could afford £8 billion on Trident when it could not afford £3 million on *HMS Endurance* 'to meet a threat that is facing us today', Nott replied 'these issues are too important to be diverted into a discussion on "HMS Endurance"'.

Too late was it realized that sovereign British territory was about to be seized by a foreign power. There was time only for frantic but futile diplomatic activity. The Government only became convinced that British territory was indeed about to seized just two days before it happened. Up to this point there had been some Cassandras in the intelligence community but the general view was disbelief that Argentine would take such a drastic step. There was a greater readiness to believe in a campaign of graduated pressure. Had Argentina adopted such an approach it might actually have been in a better position: Britain would have been put on the spot without being provoked into a major military response. (Argentina did not follow such a course because it feared this would encourage British cooperation with Argentina's main local rival, Chile.)

Even when the Government became aware of the inpending crisis, however, it is surprising that it made no ultimatum, nor warned the Argentine Government of the likely consequences of its action. Caught by disbelief and inadequate intelligence the Government could not bring itself to threaten a response which it was not sure it could muster. All that was done was to request the United States to put pressure on Buenos Aires to hold back. A call from President Reagan to General Galtieri on the eve of the actual invasion achieved nothing. By the time their conversation took place it was too late to turn the invasion off.

4 April's Diplomacy

The Argentinians have been claiming for 200 years that they own those islands. If they own those islands, then moving troops into them is not armed aggression.
Mrs Jeanne Kirkpatrick, US Ambassador to the United Nations

Haig went out of his way several times in the following weeks to promise me that there would be no repeat of Suez. Given the possible parallels, I do not think his assurances were otiose.
Sir Nicholas Henderson, British Ambassador in Washington

Argentina expected a muted and embarrassed British response: it was mistaken. Nothing could turn the Falkland Islands themselves into some great strategic and economic asset, but the circumstances of their loss turned their recapture into a popular cause. Here was a clear act of aggression and a disregard of the principle of peaceful settlement of inter-national disputes. The victims were clearly British while the perpetrators were fascistic and, fortunately, white and not too wretched. Moreover, there was a need to avenge what Lord Carrington described, in his resignation as Foreign Secretary, as a 'national humiliation'.

The option of a solely non-military response was not seriously considered, though it was recognized from the start that any military operation was likely to be hazardous and without guarantee of success. There were no contingency plans in the Ministry of Defence for an operation of this sort. Since the mid-1960s it had been assumed that Britain would never again seek to apply military force on a substantial scale outside the NATO area. Admiral Sir Henry Leach, the First Sea Lord, managed at a critical moment to persuade the cabinet that military options were available. He also correctly suggested that any options that were to have any chance of success would require all the capabilities that could be effectively transported to the South Atlantic. Accordingly the most substantial possible task force was put together in the quickest possible time and sent on its way to create an option for eventual military action and, in the first instance, to add weight to British diplomacy. A large naval task force would take a number of weeks to reach the South Atlantic; there was more time than is normally available on these occasions to explore diplomatic solutions to the crisis. To encourage a peaceful withdrawal, Britain sought to maximize pressure on Argentina.

Diplomatic activity was also important, however, in gaining international and domestic support for Britain's position. If it did prove necessary to resort to military action it was important to be able to demonstrate that Britain was the aggrieved party, that Britain had been reasonable in any negotiations and was therefore justified now in taking drastic steps.

The pressure began at the United Nations, where the Security Council passed Resolution 502 on 3 April. This determined that there had been a 'breach of the peace in the region' and demanded 'an immediate cessation of hostilities' and 'an immediate withdrawal of all Argentine forces from the Falkland Islands (Islas Malvinas)'. The Resolution concluded with a call to both sides to seek a diplomatic settlement. Britain would have preferred condemnation of Argentina as an aggressor and a firm insistence on a return to the status quo ante, but the United States was unhappy with both propositions. None the less, it was a considerable diplomatic triumph, providing subsequent British actions with a legitimacy that they might have otherwise lacked. Coupled with Article 51 of the UN Charter which allows for the 'inherent right of individual or collective self-defence if an armed attack occurs against a member of the United Nations', Britain could justify the later use of armed force.

Of the 15 members of the Security Council only Panama voted against. A Soviet vote against would have been a veto, but Moscow decided to abstain along with the two other Communist states, China and Poland. Spain, which has its own territorial dispute with Britain over Gibraltar as well as close connections with its old Latin American colonies, also abstained. All the other members voted in favour. These included a number of non-aligned states who in the past had shown sympathy to Argentine claims over the Falklands. However, as the then British Ambassador to the United Nations, Sir Anthony Parsons, has commented, they also 'have a healthy antipathy to the use of force to settle political problems'. In getting this Resolution passed the Foreign Office redeemed itself (to some extent) in the Prime Minister's eyes.

On 9 April the European Community's Council of Ministers agreed to economic sanctions against Argentina, surprising themselves by their alacrity and unanimity. (Needless to say, this did not set a pattern for future decision-making on the matter.) The sanctions included a six-week import ban and a suspension of trade preferences. Other friendly nations followed with their own sanctions. Britain's own trade embargo had been imposed three days earlier. Britain's imports from Argentina in 1981 were worth £137 million, and exports £161 million, making the country one of Britain's best markets in Latin America. In the first few months of 1982 there had been a decline in trade between the two countries. Britain froze Argentine financial assets in Britain as one of the first measures in response to the invasion, along with the breaking of diplomatic relations.

Within its own regional organization, the Rio Treaty of the Organization of American States, Argentina secured strong rhetorical support when it met on 26 April. (It was significant that the meeting was convened against the wishes of the United States for the first time since the Treaty's formation.) This meeting decided that British action represented an external threat to the peace and security of the Americas and recognized Argentine sovereignty over the disputed islands. The vote was helped by the British re-occupation of South Georgia the previous day. However, no sanctions against Britain were requested or applied (Argentina's own sanctions were never as strict as the corresponding British sanctions because of the need to secure imports of key spare parts). Also, in some Latin American states support for Argentina was lukewarm. Chile, Colombia, Costa Rica and the United States all abstained at the Rio Treaty meeting. Colombia's President changed soon afterwards, however, and by the time the Treaty nations met again Colombia was ready to support Argentina. Chile, with its long-standing rivalry with Argentina, was a virtual ally of Britain. It provided intelligence and some other facilities (to an extent which is still shrouded in secrecy) but, being aware of the general regional backing for its neighbour, it did not consider opening up a second front.

The Haig mediation

These various moves helped Britain apply the pressure but the most critical nation was the United States. Washington, however, was embarrassed at a quarrel between two allies. It was not for nothing that Britain's relationship with the United States was known as 'special'. On the other hand Argentina was playing a larger role in US Latin American policy and there were strong urgings within the Reagan Administration that Argentina, along with other Latin American states who could be expected to demonstrate regional solidarity, should not be alienated by an immediate show of support for Britain. Washington's Ambassador to the United Nations, Mrs Jeane Kirkpatrick, even went to a dinner at the Argentine Embassy on the day of the invasion.

When pressed in the early days of April by Britain to condemn Argentina vigorously and withdraw its Ambassador, the United States did neither but chose a cautious path. Secretary of State Alexander Haig explained:

While my sympathy was with the British, I believed that the most practical expression of that sympathy would be impartial United States mediation in the dispute. The honest broker must, above all, be neutral.

President Reagan offered Haig to both sides as a mediator and they accepted. They had little choice. It is perhaps a shame that they had not attempted more active mediation in the days just before the Argentine occupation, when such efforts might have succeeded.

Haig's involvement suited the Argentine strategy more than the British. While there were doubts in Buenos Aires as to whether they could hold on to the gains they had recently made through military actions, at least by ensuring that the United States focused on the problem there was hope of putting pressure on Britain to adopt a more reasonable approach to the long-term future of the islands. The United States was seen in Buenos Aires as a counter-weight to the Falkland Islands lobby, and possibly even welcomed as such by the Foreign Office.

Britain would naturally have preferred an unequivocal statement of support for its stand as both the aggrieved in the dispute and as a special ally. The activities of the 'Latin lobby' inside the US Administration did not ease Britain's irritation. It was frustrating to watch a display of American even-handedness between aggressor and aggrieved. There was some feeling that this hid from Buenos Aires the extent of its isolation, without producing commensurate benefits in the process of mediation.

In the event, Haig's mission was ineffectual. Apparently attempting to emulate the successes of his former patron Dr Henry Kissinger, he shuttled backwards and forwards between the warring parties. However he lacked a feel for the underlying issues, took too long to come up with his own proposals for settling the dispute and lacked the diplomatic skills to bridge the gaps in the stated positions of the two sides. Whatever the hopes in Buenos Aires, Haig was unable to put pressure on the British Prime Minister to be conciliatory. She saw no reason to compromise when Argentina had been the aggressor. When this resolve was communicated to the Argentine leaders they were unimpressed. Haig later complained that decision-making in the Junta was complicated and the outcomes inconsistent.

Because the military outcome of a clash of arms was uncertain neither side felt itself under pressure to abandon its basic principles, and Haig could find no formula to enable the issues to be fudged. Britain hinted at flexibility in future negotiations and began to equivocate over the extent to which the islanders' wishes would be 'paramount' but could not promise that future negotiations would reach the conclusion desired by Argentina; Argentina promised to respect and improve the islanders' current way of life. Neither side could concede anything on the fundamental principle of sovereignty. Britain demanded a return to the status quo ante; Argentina insisted on recognition of the new status quo.

For the United States, its later relations with Latin America would probably have been better if there had been immediate support for Britain. When Washington eventually tilted in London's direction on 30 April, many in Buenos Aires concluded that the shuttle diplomacy had been an elaborate cover while the British task force sailed to the South Atlantic, and that Haig had been serving the British war effort all along. In terms of a peaceful settlement of the crisis, Haig used up the negotiating time made available by the slow passage of the British task force to the South Atlantic whereas an early American tilt in Britain's direction might have brought home to the Junta the reality of its diplomatic position. Although the British Government was not pleased with a month's delay before Haig finally came down on its behalf, in practice this further strengthened Britain's position as the conflict moved into a more vicious phase. Now Haig not only offered the practical help of economic sanctions against Argentina and military assistance to Britain, he also blamed Argentina for the failure of the negotiations as well as the original aggression:

in light of Argentina's failure to accept a compromise, we must take concrete steps to underscore that the United States cannot and will not condone the use of unlawful force to resolve disputes.

5 The Campaign

May I make it perfectly clear that the worry that I live with hourly is that attacking Argentine forces, either naval or air, may get through to ours and sink some of our ships.
Prime Minister Margaret Thatcher, House of Commons, 4 May 1982

The political and economic pressures faced by Buenos Aires were severe but resistible, given the domestic popularity of the Government's positions. Nor was there reason initially to believe that the military pressures were irresistible. Time was on Argentina's side. If Britain failed to get quick results, then its military operation would become difficult to sustain and it would be forced to retreat. By then the immediate fuss would have passed over; the international community would soon come to terms with the new situation and economic sanctions would fall into disrepair.

The British assessment was not that different. There was little confidence in economic sanctions as a means of solving the dispute, though an arms embargo would be helpful if fighting began in earnest. The international support for Britain's stance was gratifying and probably important in terms of maintaining domestic support, but could not be decisive in solving the dispute. If anything could impress the Argentine leaders, it was likely to be the military power to be faced if they failed to back down peacefully and gracefully.

On both military and diplomatic grounds, it was therefore pointless for Britain to send a token force. From the start the task force had to look capable in principle of re-taking the islands. But even then it was not obviously and overwhelmingly superior to the force it would meet. As no outcome could be predicted from an analysis of the balance of the forces, battle would have to be joined before either side need feel obliged to make significant concessions. Furthermore, while it was in

Argentina's interests to prevaricate, Britain could not really allow too long for diplomacy unaccompanied by military action. In May, the fighting began in earnest.

The forces

The quality of the British military response was a function of the numbers of men and material that could be transported 8,000 miles to the South Atlantic and then sustained in operational condition over an extended period. The extent to which this was achieved is one of the most remarkable logistical feats of modern times. The bulk of the task force was prepared for departure virtually over a weekend. Not only were warships fitted out and equipped but also civilian ships were transformed to take helicopters and to refuel at sea. The success of this operation was due to sheer hard work at the dockyards and other naval establishments, laws which facilitated the requisitioning and chartering of civilian ships, and detailed contingency plans drawn up for a European emergency which guided all this activity.

The task force did not quite exhaust Britain's naval resources. It did require the services of both the Royal Navy's aircraft carriers, *HMS Hermes* and *HMS Invincible*, both of its amphibious assault ships (recently reprieved from being scrapped) and practically all of the fleet auxiliaries. However, during the campaign the total number of destroyers and frigates sent to the South Atlantic was only a portion of Britain's surface fleet. Forty-four warships were involved in all, and the maximum number active at any one time was 26 (in the second half of May). This was in addition to 12 ships of the Royal Fleet auxiliary and two of the Royal Maritime Auxiliary Service. A crucial factor was the number of civilian ships which were mobilized – some 45 in total. The most celebrated were the luxury liners *Canberra* and *QE2*, which served as troopships, but others played critical roles from tankers to hospitals.

The second important factor in the logistical effort was Ascension Island, owned by Britain but normally used only by the United States. Some 3,500 miles from the Falkland Islands, it was too far back to be used as an operating base but it was invaluable as a staging post, with personnel and freight being taken there by air to continue their journey by sea. Because of the speed with which the task force had been despatched, faults could only be repaired and gaps made good when it reached Ascension with special flights from Britain and frantic activity on the island, Wideawake soon became one of the world's busiest airports.

The troops sent with the first wave of the task force were by and large made up of the highly trained specialist units – Royal Marine commandos, the Parachute battalions and the Special Air Service. They were joined later on by soldiers from the Guards Division and the Nepalese Gurkha troops, who were less well suited to the particular demands of this campaign. In all the land forces totalled some 10,000 men. The task force itself involved some 28,000 men.

The task force was most limited by the lack of air power it could carry. Deployed in the South Atlantic were 22 Sea Harriers, joined later by six more and by ten Royal Air Force Harrier GR3 combat support aircraft, and 140 sundry helicopters of which the majority were either Sea Kings or Wessex. There were none of the wide-ranging fighter aircraft that would have been found on earlier generations of aircraft carriers.

As part of the effort to compensate for this deficiency, great strides were made in the art of in-flight refueling. This was used to get Harrier GR3s to Ascension Island (and for four to fly directly on to a carrier), as well as four Vulcan bombers, Nimrod maritime surveillance aircraft and Hercules transport aircraft. The 16 Victor tankers based at Wideawake airport on Ascension Island were kept busy but their military impact was limited. As it took ten Victors to keep one Vulcan in the air for the raids on the islands, only one bomber could be used at a time. Nimrod air warning and control aircraft did not really get close to the combat zone. It was only through individual pilots being willing to fly excessive numbers of sorties and the maintenance crews attaining impressive levels of availability (of up to 90 per cent) that effective patrols could be maintained. With aircraft and helicopters of limited range and staying power, the capability that the task force missed the most was for early warning of enemy attack.

In terms of crisis management and political control the distance between London and the South Atlantic posed enormous problems. Communications were slow. They were often most difficult with the submarines, which were none the less playing a central role in British strategy.

These problems were exacerbated by deficiencies in intelligence: there was no satellite photography nor even much useful aerial reconnaissance. A steady stream of good quality communications intelligence was interrupted for a while when a former Labour minister inadvertently revealed in Parliament on 3 April (in the course of refuting a Government claim that it could not have forseen the Argentine invasion because it could not read the minds of its leaders) that the intelligence services had been reading Argentine communications – 'As well trying to read the mind of the enemy, we have been reading its telegrams for many years.' The new codes were eventually broken and this was a crucial source of information. However, not all communications could be broken and there were often delays in passing the decoded messages on to the assessment staffs. Even then, of course, without collateral information it was often hard to make sense of the material.

The Argentine forces awaiting Britain benefited from geography – home ports and air bases. Nevertheless, the islands were some 400 miles from the mainland, which meant that Argentine aircraft had to operate at the limits of their range while an awkward supply line had to be set up to service the garrison defending the newly won territory.

Argentine forces when compared with those of Britain looked impressive enough, with many weapons of comparable quality and similar type – often, embarrassingly, bought in Britain. The Navy was smaller than that of the British task force and many elements of it were of Second World War vintage. But other elements such as British destroyers, French frigates and German submarines, and much of the armament, were quite modern. In the air there was a clear advantage in numbers if not in quality with some 12O Mirages, Skyhawks, Super-Etendards and Canberras. (Here, too, great strides were made with in-flight re-fuelling.) The other advantage derived from being the defending force. By the end of April 10,000 troops – a mixture of regulars and conscripts – had been transferred to the islands and positions had been fortified.

First shots

The commander of the task force, conducting what was officially designated as Operation Corporate, was charged with bringing about the withdrawal of the Argentine forces from the Falkland Islands and re-establishing British administration there with the minimum loss of life. However,in a conflict such as this the military cannot expect to be allowed simply to defeat the enemy armed forces through whatever appear to be the most expeditious and effective means. There are political constraints on the measures that they can adopt. This was not an occasion for turning to Britain's nuclear arsenal. Direct attacks on the Argentine mainland were advocated but ruled out because of the possible impact on international opinion (and also doubts as to their effectiveness).

Even when it is intended to give the impression that only measured force is being applied, however, in practice it is not always so easy to control the use of armed force. This is especially so when facing a competent and well-equipped enemy against whom it might be too dangerous to take risks. Furthermore, while it might be advisable for the sake of public support at home and abroad to appear moderate, it is also necessary to convince the adversary of resolve. An effective display of force might extract sufficient concessions in nego-tiations to make further and more violent action unnecessary. In these ways the military found themselves under pressure to be mindful of the immediate diplomatic impact of their operations as well as their ultimate objective of re-taking the islands.

A prerequisite for most of the strategic alternatives was to blockade the defending forces to limit their reinforcement. A maritime exclusion zone of 200 miles was thus declared on 12 April, as soon as Buenos Aires could reasonably expect a nuclear submarine to have reached the area. This was turned into a total exclusion zone once the main task force arrived.

Before it reached the exclusion zone, elements of the task force were diverted to retake the dependency of South Georgia. This was not part of the original plan, but the opportunity to demonstrate military prowess, probably without interference from the Argentine Navy or Air Force because of the distance from the mainland, was too tempting. It might have been hoped that it would strengthen Secretary of State Haig's hand in his efforts to convince the Junta that Britain was prepared to take whatever action necessary. In the event the operation was almost a disaster. An advance party was helicoptered on to a glacier on which it got stuck. Two helicopters crashed trying to rescue it but a third succeeded. These mishaps were kept secret, partly so that Argentina was unaware of the loss of these assets. On 25 April a submarine was observed reinforcing the garrison. The operation was immediately brought forward. The Argentine submarine *Santa Fe* was severely damaged by missiles and depth charges from helicopters and was forced to ditch on land. Marines landed and surprised the garrison, which surrendered without much resistance, providing the desired impression of an effortless British victory. If this first operation had ended as a fiasco it could have finished the whole campaign, leaving a completely different impression from the one eventually created. In Argentina the impact of this incident was probably to increase military preparations rather than to extract concessions, although there was some hope that having regained territory Britain might now feel that honour was sufficiently satisfied to contemplate serious negotiations.

The major military problem was time. The task force could not stay in the South Atlantic indefinitely. Deteriorating weather conditions would make it more difficult to mount an operation and also to keep troops at sea without their becoming demoralized and unfit. The military instinct was therefore to concentrate from the start in preparing for a landing on the islands. The need for special forces to infiltrate the islands to build up a picture of the Argentine land forces meant it was necessary to get close to the Islands regularly. The main concern was that the Argentine Air Force and Navy should be engaged prior to a landing so as to cause the maximum attrition and therefore reduce the opposition to the eventual landing.

The first stage of the military operation came on 1 May. With a considerable effort a Vulcan bomber attacked Stanley airport early on May Day morning. This damaged the airport but not sufficiently to put it out of action fully. The attack prevented high-performance combat aircraft from using the airfield but not lighter aircraft and transports. Argentine transports managed to get through until the end, largely by taking risks flying on to an inadequate airfield at night. Reconnaissance was unsatisfactory, as a result of cloud cover and shortage of aircraft. The British were fooled by sand placed on strategic points in the runway to appear to be craters. However, this operation had the incidental effect of demonstrating a capability of attacking air bases on the Argentine mainland, which in turn led to a squadron of Mirage fighters being held back by Argentina to ward off such an attack

The sinking of the *General Belgrano*

On the same day, 1 May, there were a number of Harrier raids and naval bombardments against Argentine positions on the islands. This was designed to give the impression of an attempted landing, so as to draw out the Argentine Navy and Air Force. In particular it was hoped to attack the Argentine carrier the *25 de Mayo*. The previous day the war cabinet had given permission for a submarine to attack the carrier should it cross its patrol area as it positioned itself to launch air strikes against the task force. However, the submarine failed to find the carrier, while the carrier failed to launch its aircraft. At the end of the day the Argentine commanders concluded that no British landings were taking place and that prudence required a return to safer waters. The British commanders did not know this. They were worried by their failure to find the carrier, which they assumed to be closing on them. The only major Argentine ship they had found was the old cruiser the *General Belgrano*, escorted by two destroyers, and trailed by another British submarine, *HMS Conquerer*. The task force commanders wanted to attack this target but had to wait for a political decision to permit such an attack. By the time the decision could be taken the next day, the cruiser had turned round and was heading away from the task force.

On the assumption that it was still closing, ministers authorized an attack on the *Belgrano*. *HMS Conquerer* received the order authorizing the attack as it was transmitting its report of the change of course. The cruiser was torpedoed with the loss of 360 men in the most costly single engagement of the war.

During 2 May some progress had been made by President Belaunde of Peru with a revised and simplified version of Haig's peace plan. He had begun to negotiate the outline of an acceptable version with Argentina and was assuming that Secretary of State Haig was doing the same with British Foreign Secretary Francis Pym, who was in Washington at the time. It was assumed in Peru (and so in Argentina) that when Haig spoke he was virtually speaking for Britain. In fact Haig made slight progress with Pym who was expecting the next diplomatic effort to be led by the UN Secretary-General, the Peruvian Perez de Cuellar. Haig was confusing both sides. In the evening of 2 May President Galtieri was to put the Peruvian plan to the rest of the Junta. At the same time news of the sinking of the *Belgrano* arrived; the response was rejection of the Peruvian proposals.

The indictment developed by critics of the British Government's handling of events, such as Labour MP Tam Dalyell, starts with the assumption that the *Belgrano* was not a threat to the task force. It then moves on to search for motives other than military ones to explain the sinking. The main allegation has been that the Prime Minister wanted to scuttle the new diplomatic initiative led by Peru. The critics have put a lot of energy into demonstrating that the Government *must* have known of this promising possibility for a peace settlement, just as they *must* have known that the *Belgrano* was not a threat.

The Government for its part did not want it to be suggested that it was ill-informed when contemplating major military actions and so seized on evidence that the *Belgrano* was a threat and also that there was nothing in the Peruvian initiative at the time that could have altered its decision.

The truth is inevitably much more complex than is suggested in either the Government's or the critic's case. It is also more disturbing. Both the Government and critics assume that the Government was essentially in control of matters, and was therefore able to relate diplomatic to military activity. In particular, they assume first-rate intelligence appreciations despite the confusion of the campaign. The critics believe that intelligence-gathering gave the Government not only access to the innermost thoughts of the Argentine Junta but also made it to some degree clairvoyant about the decisions that the Junta had yet to take.

What has now become clear is that the enthusiasm on the Peruvian side for its initiative on 2 May was based on a combination of diplomatic inexperience and a misplaced assumption that American Secretary of State Alexander Haig was virtually representing the British when he spoke with Peruvian President Belaunde. As for the military action, it would seem that the British acted in the belief that the *Belgrano* was part of a general Argentine offensive against the task force. Such a general attack had indeed been ordered but it had been called off. The intelligence appreciation upon which the Government agreed to sink the cruiser was simply out of date.

One moment exemplifies the problem: a Sea Harrier from the task force chanced upon the main body of the Argentine fleet early on the morning of 2 May. It immediately flew back to warn that the enemy was approaching. This information was passed back to London to form a crucial part of the intelligence assessment upon which the decision to attack the *Belgrano* was based. But it was immediately rendered out of date. The Argentine Admiral on board the cruiser the *25 de Mayo* spotted the Harrier and became concerned that his fleet was now at risk from the Royal Navy. He ordered a withdrawal.

Whether with better intelligence the Royal Navy would have held back is not altogether certain; it welcomed an opportunity to strike a blow against the Argentine Navy. The demonstration of the power of modern submarines was underlined when it was announced a few days later that any Argentine warships or aircraft found further than 12 miles from the Argentine coast would be treated as hostile. No Argentine surface warships took up the challenge, though a number of patrol boats and supply ships were caught attempting to break the blockade. All Argentina could do was to avenge the loss of the *General Belgrano*. The destroyer *HMS Sheffield* was surprised on 4 May by an air-launched Exocet missile. Twenty sailors were killed, and the ship abandoned to sink. At the time, the main diplomatic cost of the *Belgrano* incident was not seen in the loss of the Peruvian initiative – which was sustained until the 7 May – but in the loss of international political support for Britain's case. The victim was just outside the 200-mile exclusion zone. Although Britain had been very careful not to suggest that this was a combat-inclusive zone it had been widely understood as such. Such a dramatic transformation of the crisis led to accusations of unwarranted escalation. Secretary of State Haig made known to Britain his concern that action such as this was alienating Latin America and threatening the Western position on the continent.

Diplomatic impact

While the sinking of the *Belgrano* was mounted for military reasons, the consequences were as much political as military. It put the Argentine Junta in no mood to accept the Peruvian initiative. But by no means is it clear that the initiative would have been successful, given that the form it was in at the time was unacceptable to Britain. What is clear is that the attack on the *Belgrano* weakened Britain's international standing.

The Peruvian initiative was based on the original Haig proposals. The reason there had been a chance it might have been accepted by Argentina on 2 May was that the proposals had been modified in Peruvian-Argentine discussions on that day. This had led to a watering down of the provision for a final settlement to take account of the wishes of the islanders. At the time the Junta met after the sinking of the *Belgrano* only the Foreign Secretary visiting Haig in Washington was aware of the initiative, which he considered underdeveloped and without obvious prospects. It was only after the sinking of the

Belgrano and then the attack on *HMS Sheffield* that the British Government began to take these ideas seriously.

All of a sudden the realities of warfare had come rushing in on the war cabinet. In the immediate aftermath of the *Belgrano* incident the Foreign Secretary had felt obliged to issue a reassurance that there was no desire to inflict a military humiliation on Argentina. Then the loss of one of the Royal Navy's most powerful warships underlined the risks that the professionals had warned faced the task force when they came in range of Argentine air power.. The sudden escalation in the fighting had many in the international community distinctly uneasy about continuing with unequivocal support for Britain and more determined than ever to negotiate a cease-fire.

Britain's international support did not crumble, but it certainly began to erode. The Irish Government chose to criticize Britain for its action and take a call for an immediate cease-fire to the UN Security Council. To British relief the Council was resistant to this request as the Secretary-General was just beginning to get involved in the negotiations and there was concern that another major Security Council debate could undermine his efforts. Within the EEC Ireland also argued that the sanctions against Argentina should be discontinued forthwith. There were clear expressions of concern from Germany and Denmark. Italy which has close connections with Argentina was particularly unhappy. When the question of the renewal of sanctions came up at a meeting of foreign ministers in Luxembourg on 16 May, there was no agreement. The next day a compromise was agreed by which sanctions would be renewed weekly on a voluntary basis. Italy and Ireland opted out. Although as a matter of principle Britain's main European allies France and Germany maintained firm support, sympathy for Britain was not helped by a coincidental hard line taken by Mrs Thatcher on the question of the Community budget, where she found herself (neither for the first nor the last time) in a minority of one.

That Britain's position did not crumble was largely due to the fact that for much of the first half of May it did seem to be taking attempts to reach a negotiated solution seriously. After the shock of the *Belgrano* and the *Sheffield*, the Government adopted a more conciliatory attitude than it had been prepared to adopt before or was to be prepared to adopt later. On 6 May the Government accepted a version of the Peruvian proposals which reaffirmed the importance of the wishes of the islanders but did accept an interim administration made up of a small group of countries excluding Britain to supervise the withdrawal of Argentine forces and be involved in negotiations for a 'definitive agreement on the status of the islands'. This was the most that the British Government was ever prepared to offer. By this time, however, Argentina was no longer interested.

Argentina was now putting more faith in the United Nations. On the eventful day of 2 May, the UN Secretary-General, Perez de Cuellar, had put forward proposals of his own to Foreign Secretary Francis Pym and to the Argentine representative to the UN. Later that week both countries indicated their willingness to proceed on the basis of his ideas, which built on some of the earlier proposals. As developed in intensive consultations with the two states' Ambassadors to the UN, these provisions envisaged a temporary UN Administration for the islands and negotiations for a final settlement to be carried out under the auspices of the Secretary-General. Optimism grew when it appeared that Buenos Aires had conceded that the outcome of the talks need not be a predetermined transfer of sovereignty.

Over the weekend of 15 and 16 May Sir Anthony Parsons, the British Ambassador to the UN who had been engaged in the negotiations, returned to London to discuss matters with the Prime Minister and her colleagues. Afterwards he went back to New York and presented the final British position to the Secretary-General. The Argentine position, communicated the next day, 18 May, was taken to amount to a rejection. The Junta could not bring itself to make an unequivocal concession on the open-ended nature of the talks. So these negotiations too had failed, although the gap now was narrower than before. Britain was prepared to see some Argentine involvement in the running of the islands but was insistent that the democratic institutions of the islands should be revived, a condition rejected by Argentina who feared that the islanders would thus make clear their aversion to any transfer of sovereignty to Argentina. Argentina also wanted freedom of access to the Falklands during the interim period, which would have allowed them to change the demographic base of the islands. Lastly, Argentina wanted to include the dependencies in the arrangement. This too Britain refused to accept (although in the past Britain had accepted that there was some logic in treating all the various islands as a unity).

After the breakdown of the UN talks Panama obtained a Security Council debate. The Irish proposed a cease-fire with a re-opening of negotiations. It was Britain's main concern throughout the negotiations that a cease-fire would favour Argentina as it was much better placed to hold its military position over the long term. The British task force would start to face problems if the campaign went into a fourth month, so a cease-fire without an Argentine withdrawal as required in Resolution 502, combined with protracted negotiations, could see the steady erosion of Britain's bargaining position. When Britain made its final offers at the end of both the Peruvian and the Secretary-General's initiatives, it did so with a requirement that a definitive Argentine response come within 48 hours. Faced with these concerns the Security Council was persuaded that it was unwise to press for a cease-fire. Instead it was decided in Resolution 505 to ask the Secretary-General to make one last attempt at mediation before re-convening to consider alternative courses of action. The Secretary-General tried and, as expected, failed.

By the time Resolution 505 was passed by the Security Council, however, the military situation had changed yet again. British forces had now landed on the Falkland Islands.

The landing

For the first three weeks of May the task force was preparing itself to mount a landing. The landing was not held back in order to allow diplomacy to run its course. The three weeks were required for some of the ships carrying critical supplies to reach the South Atlantic, for patrols to be inserted on to the islands to recconnoitre Argentine positions and then report back, and for development of plans for the landing. However, the knowledge that preparations were almost complete will have influenced the attitude taken by the Government to the last stages of the Perez de Cuellar initiative which was concluded on 19 May, and in particular will have lain behind the demand for a definitive Argentine response within 48 hours rather than permitting any prevarication.

Those involved in the planning were well aware of the hazards of trying to land sufficient men, stores and equipment to be able to fight the initial stages of a campaign to dislodge Argentine forces. At the 'counsel of war' at Ascension Island in mid-April, those responsible for the landing had pressed for every effort to be made to ensure that it would not have to be undertaken in the face of determined assaults by the Argentine Navy and Air Force.

The sinking of the *Belgrano* did seem to have discouraged the Argentine Navy from venturing too far from its home ports. The anticipated large-scale naval battle never materialized. Of the Argentine submarines, one of the old ones was cannibalized for its twin which was caught at South Georgia. Of the two modern German submarines little was seen. There were rumours of problems in their operation. Once Sea Kings attacked what might have been a submarine with no evident results. Throughout the campaign the task force warships continued to mount the most intensive anti-submarine operations, without ever quite knowing whether or not they were necessary.

The air strategy was to destroy Argentine air resources wherever possible. This was less successful. On 1 May, a Sea Harrier shot down a Mirage while others successfully took on two Canberras. Thereafter the Argentine Air Force avoided dogfights with the Sea Harriers to conserve resources for a British landing. On being spotted by Harriers, Argentine aircraft returned home. More success was achieved by a commando raid on a small airstrip at Pebble Island on 15 May. Eleven aircraft, mainly light ground-attack Pucaras, were destroyed. However, despite these and a few other losses, the bulk of the Argentine Air Force was still intact.

Those planning an eventual landing were extremely unhappy at the prospect of carrying out such an operation before the air battle had been clearly won. Yet it became clear that the Argentine air force was avoiding action until the landings. There were calls to deal with the problem by attacking the air bases on the Argentine mainland. This was considered and was certainly feared by Argentina. However, in addition to the practical problems involved in such an attack – knocking out runways is not the easiest of tasks at the best of times as the raid on Stanley airfield had demonstrated – there were political problems. A raid on Argentine territory would have been viewed as a major escalation and was ruled out for this reason.

By mid-May there were no signs that the military pressure exerted thus far was encouraging Argentine compromise on the sovereignty issue. There was no reason to believe that the state of the garrison on the island was dire, or that it had less staying power than the task force. Only one Harrier had been lost in combat (attacking Stanley) but two others and three helicopters had been lost in accidents. This plus the destruction of *HMS Sheffield* created the prospect of gradual attrition that would lower morale. The greatest problem was of sustaining the task force in increasingly stormy and inclement weather over an extended period. Stuck on board ships the soldiers would lose combat readiness. Options to harass the enemy by small-scale raids or even troop landings on remote parts of the islands were thought not to inconvenience the enemy sufficiently.

There was little choice but to attempt a landing. Those with a knowledge of the history of British amphibious landings could feel nothing but trepidation: especially without command of the air. The calculation was made that, in military terms, substantial losses were tolerable if the land forces could establish a beachhead. On 21 May a dawn landing was made at Port San Carlos Water off the Falkland Sound, which divides the two main islands, just to the west of East Falkland, 50 miles from Stanley. The landing succeeded beyond the expectations of the British command.

It was important that no enemy forces were sufficiently close to provide opposition. At the start of May, at the earliest possible opportunity, special forces had been landed on the islands to keep a close watch on Argentine positions. The islands offered many alternative landing sites, most of which would be undefended. However, because of the lack of an internal road network and the limited number of heavy-lift helicopters, it had to be feasible to move forces onwards to Stanley. One advantage of San Carlos Water was that the Argentine command probably assumed it was too far away for British forces. The other advantage was that the layout of the bay made it very difficult to mount air attacks on the landing forces. With the attacking aircraft coming from the west, they would have first to pass a Harrier cordon, then a picket line of ships with a variety of anti-air defenses and eventually the anti-aircraft weapons of the ground forces. The disadvantage was that many warships would have to sit for a number of days in highly vulnerable positions. A significant advantage lay in the fact that there was only one entrance to San Carlos Water and *Exocet* would be unable to acquire targets against the surrounding land mass. Nor was there much risk of submarines, and even aircraft armed with iron bombs, cannon and rockets found it difficult to attack effectively. This is one reason why most of the ships connected with the landing remained inside San Carlos Water even in daylight. The ships would probably have been most vulnerable to anti-ship mines but this threat did not materialize.

With the help of a series of diversionary raids, surprise was achieved. By the time Argentine forces had realized what was going on, three separate beachheads had been established and 4,000 men were ashore. Every effort had been made to encourage the Argentine commanders to believe that this was a diversion and the main landing was still to take place nearer Stanley, and this effort had some success. Eventually, the air raids came. In the intensive duels four ships – two frigates, a destroyer and one merchantman (the *Atlantic Conveyor*) – were lost. Contrary to repeated claims from Buenos Aires, neither aircraft carrier was hit, nor was the most valuable target to venture into Falkland Sound, the troopship *Canberra*. An Exocet missile was diverted on to the *Atlantic Conveyor* from the carrier *HMS Invincible* by the use of chaff, one of a number of countermeasures that were developed against this missile during the campaign. Later on, a ground-launched Exocet from Stanley struck *HMS Glamorgan* a glancing blow.

The loss of the *Atlantic Conveyor* turned out to be a more serious loss in material terms than those of the warships for she was carrying equipment (including three *Chinook* helicopters) critical to the land campaign. The loss of these helicopters hampered subsequent British operations. It was a major strategic error of the Argentine forces not to direct more of their effort against the Royal Fleet Auxiliaries and the merchant ships carrying the essential back-up for the armed forces instead of being distracted by the high-profile targets presented by the warships.

The Argentine Air Force suffered dreadful attrition. The pilots flew bravely and skilfully with, at times, barely a one in two chance of survival. In the three days of 21 May to 24 May up to 40 aircraft were lost. The effort left the Argentine Air Force severely depleted and exhausted. The only aircraft able to bother the British ground forces were the Pucaras still on the islands. Towards the end of the campaign, aircraft were mustered for a major effort on 8 June. This succeeded in inflicting the heaviest British casualties of the war on two landing ships in Port Fitzroy.

The land campaign which followed was neither as spectacular nor as interesting to those addicted to modern technology. Air power played a limited role on either side, conditions were unconducive to armoured warfare and there was an absence of urban sprawl and modern roadways. The British task was to dislodge a well-armed enemy from entrenched positions. The methods were not dissimilar to those of the Great War – artillery bombardment combined with determined infantry assaults on vulnerable points with a hope that surprise, training and morale could compensate for the natural advantages accruing to the defence. Formulas offering guidance on the necessary numerical superiority for a successful offence were irrelevant simply because they could not be met. (Those involved would not recommend discarding them in the future.) The last major raid by Argentine Skyhawks was made against Brigadier Thompson's headquarters on 13 June. A number of bombs dropped close to the headquarters and three helicopters parked nearby were destroyed but there were no casualties. Canberras were also used for attacks until close to the end of the campaign. They had some near misses but again caused no casualties.

As stores were unloaded at Port San Carlos, advance patrols determined enemy dispositions. The time taken to consolidate the positions at San Carlos worried politicians in London who wanted relief from reports of British troops and ships being attacked by the Argentine Air Force. Politicians are not readily appreciative of logistical problems. There was pressure to mount an early attack on the nearest Argentine positions which were at the settlements of Goose Green and Darwin. On 28 May 600 men of the 2nd Parachute Batallion took on 1,000 Argentine troops. For a while Pucara and Aermacchis aircraft from airstrips around the Falklands controlled the skies. A British helicopter was shot down, and with helicopters already in short supply no more could be put at risk until this threat was eased. This could not be done while Harriers were boxed in at sea by bad weather. Eventually the British were able to obtain air superiority. Argentine troops fought fiercely at first but became demoralized by their inability to hold on to forward positions and then later by the arrival of British aircraft. The battle has become well known for the heroic but possibly unnecessary death of the commanding officer, Colonel 'H' Jones, as he sought to inject momentum into an attack which had ground to a halt, for which he earned a posthumous VC, and for the complaint that a 'leak' of British intentions to attack broadcast through the BBC World Service had provided an opportunity for the Argentine garrison to be reinforced. What is also interesting, however, is the relatively small number of troops committed by Britain to an action that as the first major land engagement could be expected to shape political expectations as to the likely outcome of later confrontations, and as such could also have a severe impact on the morale of the losing side. Some of the military commanders would have preferred to press on to the main objective – the Argentine garrison at the capital, Stanley – and not divert energies to Goose Green to which insufficient resources were then assigned. However, in a conflict where every encounter was of great sensitivity, once it had been decided to take the settlements it was vital that they be won.

The Argentine command had not expected an attack from the west. It had anticipated a landing reasonably close to Stanley to either the north or the south and had prepared accordingly, for example by laying minefields astride the likely attack route. Now hasty adjustments were required, including some frantic mine-laying. Another change was to move troops from Mount Kent, some five miles inland from Stanley, to reinforce the garrison at Goose Green just before the battle.

When it was realized that Mount Kent had been vacated Royal Marines moved forward in appalling conditions to occupy it. Mount Kent was a good jumping-off place for an offensive against Stanley because it dominated all the other ground. Moreover once troops were there in numbers they would be difficult to dislodge because the terrain suited defensive action. However the first troops to arrive were few in number, lacked fire support and were remote from the rest of the Brigade. If the Argentine command had organized a counter-attack (which it was extraordinarily reluctant to do throughout the campaign) then these first Marines could have been given little support. The troops holding the mountain were bitterly exposed to the elements. It required the use of scarce helicopter resources to attend to their needs. This, plus the fact that three valuable Chinook heavy-lift helicopters had been lost on the *Atlantic Conveyor*, created a helicopter shortage. However, Mount Kent provided an excellent vantage point and securing it helped convince the Argentine command that it was being pushed back into Stanley for the critical battle.

The shortage of helicopters had important consequences for the 3,000 men of the Fifth Infantry Brigade who had now arrived in San Carlos. To the new arrivals was added the Second Battalion Parachute Regiment now at Goose Green. Brigadier Wilson, now in Command of Fifth Brigade, ordered the paras to walk to Bluff Cove (just to the south of Stanley). However, instead of doing this the paras telephoned one of the local residents who informed them that Bluff Cove was not occupied by Argentine troops. On the basis of this intelligence the paras hijacked the only Chinook heavy-lift helicopter still available, crammed 80 men into it and flew to Bluff Cove. The remainder of 2nd Para was quickly moved by helicopter to join their colleagues.

As a result of this initiative an advance guard had been established, but in a highly vulnerable position and without obvious means of support. When General Moore, in charge of Land Forces, discovered what had happed he was obliged to reinforce with the rest of Fifth Brigade as soon as possible. On two successive nights *Fearless* and *Intrepid* moved the Scots Guards and parts of the Welsh Guards to Fitzroy, close by Bluff Cove, by transferring them to landing craft at sea. Unfortunately, before the move of all troops could be completed an order came from Northwood that neither *Fearless* nor *Intrepid* should be used again in this way as they were too important to put at risk.

The other troops journeyed to Fitzroy by various means. Ghurkas came in the *Monsoomen* (a local motor vessel) and by landing craft. Two troops of Blues and Royals motored with Third Brigade to the Mount Kent area and then one was detached to motor on to Bluff Cove. Welsh Guards were moved by Landing Ships. At the last stage on 8 June two landing Ships, *Sir Tristram* and *Sir Galahad*, arrived at Port Fitzroy in clear daylight to the surprise of those already there and then failed to disembark as expeditiously as the situation demanded. They were spotted. An Argentine air attack was launched and the two ships were hit, leaving 50 men dead and many more badly wounded.

Late diplomacy and final battles

When the United Nations Security Council met again on 2 June to consider the implications of the failure of the Secretary-General's final attempt at negotiation, a cease-fire resolution was proposed by Spain and Panama. This was innocuous enough for many of the non-aligned nations who had supported Britain in the past to feel obliged to endorse. Britain vetoed the resolution along with the United States. By this time Britain's military position was sufficiently strong for the international reaction to be less important. At any rate, Britain was let off the hook by a strange performance by the US Ambassador, who, after voting with Britain, asked for it to be recorded that if the US could change its vote then it would abstain. This evidence of confusion in the US Administration captured the media attention. After this particular episode there was no more serious diplomatic activity as the matter was evidently coming to a military conclusion. When this conclusion came, Israeli action in Lebanon had become the new preoccupation of the international community.

On the islands themselves land forces were now in position around Stanley for the campaign's finale. Argentine defences were based on the high ground on the outskirts of Stanley overlooking one of the islands' few roads. They had made the erroneous assumption that the British would launch their main attack along this road, which led into the capital. Instead, the defending forces were unhinged by a series of night-time attacks on their exposed flanks. The battles were sharp, with stubborn Argentine resistance in some cases and disarray elsewhere. The loss of the defensive perimeter and the wearing down caused by intense bombardment from the sea as well as land (6,000 shells over the last 12 hours) took its toll. On 14 June white flags went up and the next day General Mario Menendez, commander of the Argentine garrison, surrendered on behalf of all his forces on the Falkland Islands.

6 The Aftermath

I do not intend to negotiate on the sovereignty of the islands in any way, except with those who live there. That is my fervent belief.
Prime Minister Margaret Thatcher, House of
Commons, 15 June 1982

Having recaptured the Falklands, Britain was now obliged to defend them against a further Argentine attempt at occupation, either official or unofficial. Soon the sort of military commitments that would have been deemed preposterous in all considerations of Falklands policy prior to April 1982 became accepted as inevitable. Thousands of troops were to be based on the islands, threatening to overwhelm the local civilian population. Taking advantage of the favourable political climate, the Ministry of Defence argued for a major programme of capital investment to make it possible to reduce the level of the garrison. The single most important item was the construction of an airfield with an 8,500 foot runway to allow for the landing of wide-bodied jets (and so speedy reinforcement in a crisis). The cost of the airfield and navigational aids was put in 1987 at £319 million. This made it possible to reduce the annual running costs for the garrison from some £200 million just after the conclusion of the war to around half that amount. The bulk of those costs remain fuel for shipping and aircraft. By the mid-1980s the costs of the war, the replacement of lost equipment, the replenishment of stores and the development and maintenance of the garrison had come to something like £1.5 million per islander per year; by the end of the decade this figure will rise to some £2 million.

Although in late 1983 the Argentine military government was replaced by the democratically elected President Alfonsin, who appeared to have little interest in further belligerence, his Government refused to end hostilities. This, along with the possibility of his replacement by a less moderate government or unauthorized action against the Falklands by hard-line elements, was used to justify the continued British presence on the islands.

Following Alfonsin's election, there was interest in Britain in seeking to improve relations between the two countries, but the possibilities were limited by the refusal of the Prime Minister to contemplate discussion of sovereignty. As early as November 1982 the United Nations General Assembly had urged a resumption of talks between the two countries to resolve the dispute. It was recognized by many that, having militarily occupied the islands it would take time before an Argentine return, however legal, could easily be contemplated by the islanders. As time passed and the dust settled the view gained ground that the costs of the garrison, the need to bolster civilian government in Buenos Aires, the continued Argentine claim and the logic of the geo-political situation all argued for some sort of Anglo-Argentine dialogue on the future status of the islands. The United States, anxious to repair the damage done to its relations with Latin America, argued for it from early on. Gradually opposition leaders in Britain made the case too. Privately many within the services, Whitehall and the Government were also prepared to acknowledge the force of the argument. However, even if throughout the whole country there was a minority of only one against even contemplating, by whatever arrangement, a transfer of sovereignty to Argentina, so long as that one was the Prime Minister, nothing would happen.

In 1984 Anglo-Argentine talks were arranged in Berne in Switzerland, but they collapsed when the British delegation claimed that the Argentine side had broken the agreed rules, which had been to talk about all aspects of bilateral relations *other* than the sovereignty of the Falkland Islands. In July 1985 Britain lifted the trade embargo that had been in force since the start of the conflict.

As a result of the garrison, life on the islands was transformed. With an international airport and steadily improving roads and other facilities, the economy began to recover from the apparently irreversible downward trend of the decades pre-1982. The most important shift was in the impact of fishing. In the early 1980s a substantial squid stock, including the valuable Illex species, was discovered in the South Western Atlantic. In 1983 around 200 vessels fished in Falklands waters; by 1987 the number had grown to 700. Concern soon grew that the increased amount of fishing would begin to threaten stocks. Tentatively cooperation was sought with Argentina but eventually it was decided that Argentina saw the issue largely in terms of an opportunity to reinforce her own claims to the relevant waters. As it became apparent that multilateral agreements on conserving fish stocks in the area would not be obtained, in October 1986 Britain imposed a Falkland Islands Conservation and Management Zone of 150 miles radius from the islands to take effect from February 1987. This would require those fishing in the area to obtain a licence from the Falkland Islands Government. One of the unexpected results of the establishment of this zone was the major increase in island revenue resulting from the licence fees. It was forecast in 1987 that the Government budget for that year could reach £30 million (compared with pre-1982 budgets of £1 million) largely as a result of fishing licence revenues.

The revival of the Falklands economy has also led to a revival in its population. The November 1986 census showed a population of 1,916. The census showed that the proportion of native-born islanders – Kelpers – had declined to 67 per cent, and also that the historic trend to concentrate in the capital, with a decline in the numbers living in the 'Camp', had continued. Stanley's population was 1,232 while the Camp had declined to 653.

One interesting development of the revival of the economy is that it appears to be making many of the Islanders appreciate the familiar Whitehall argument that some sort of agreement with Argentina could make a substantial difference to the islands' prosperity. Much more money could be obtained from fishing licences if there were cooperation with Argentina in exploiting a stretch of ocean to the north of the islands currently not being patrolled by either country. While there is still little interest in a constitutional link with Argentina, the recognition of the potential of the islands has brought at least a readiness to start loosening the ties with and dependence upon Britain.

Military lessons

No sooner had the British task force set out in early April 1982 than speculation began concerning what might be learned from any future engagements about the performance of modern weapons in combat. There was particular interest in the possibility of combat between the British and Argentine navies as there has been a marked lack of major sea engagements since 1945. In the event the Argentine Navy did not venture out of port following the destruction of the *Belgrano* and the expected naval warfare did not materialize. The major threat to British warships came from land-based aircraft.

During the conflict there was a substantial amount of commentary on the performance of individual systems, such as Sea Wolf in providing point defence against Exocet and the relative successes of other air defence systems – Sea Dart, Rapier and Blowpipe in particular. Gaps in British capabilities – such as a lack of airborne early warning (which was later confirmed) – were also identified. Lastly, there was a certain amount of comment on warship design stimulated by the fate of those that were sunk. The problems with containing fire on board ship were illustrated in a particularly unpleasant way.

After the war it became clear that not all of the early speculation had been based on accurate information – for example, the widespread assumption that it had been the Tigerfish torpedo that had sunk the *Belgrano*. Also some of the early comment had been based on a lack of sensitivity to operational conditions. Nevertheless, many of the issues raised during the campaign were pursued and some new ones were also examined in the large number of books and articles on the conflict which were soon being published.

A number of factors limit the conclusions that can be drawn from any exercise of this kind, some of which are relevant to almost any war. There are inevitable problems with the accurate reporting of the key events. This is particularly notable with aircraft 'kills' where the same aircraft is often claimed by a number of attacking units. There were not always a sufficient number of comparable encounters to make possible generalizations. When Mirage and Harrier aircraft regularly met in comparable conditions then it was possible to say which was superior; but when a missile scores a 'one-off' hit against a ship the explanation may well have to be sought in the unique features of that particular engagement. The number of particular systems lost or the number of 'kills' achieved does not necessarily mean a great deal without some idea as to attrition rates – how often were those systems put at risk and how many missiles had to be fired for each success.

Easy reputations can be made by spectacular successes. Exocet is a case in point. Its dramatic entry into the war gave it a reputation for invincibility that was not wholly warranted. Other systems can be flattered by circumstances. An enemy aircraft might prove to be an easy target if it is continually being confronted at the limits of its range. But circumstances can also demean – such as when enemy tactics have to be specially designed to avoid a particular weapon, as may have been the case with Sea Dart. This air defence weapon for warships was well known to the Argentine forces as they had purchased it themselves from Britain. Their aircraft therefore recognized the Sea Dart threat when attacking British warships and flew at an altitude that was sub-optimal for releasing their bombs.

There was inevitably more interest in the performance of the most advanced weapons, but it is always the case that armed forces contain a mixture of the old and the new and so the capacities of older systems dare not be ignored. Obsolescence turns out also to be a function of circumstance – a 4.5-inch gun shot down a Skyhawk. Air attack is no occasion for sophisticated disdain of primitive weapons.

In addition there was a tendency to be obsessed by the 'teeth' to the neglect of the 'tail'. The importance of logistics and command and control were amply illustrated in the Falklands, but these aspects lack the glamour of the advanced weaponry. Moreover factors of skill, training and improvisation can be as important in performance as the innate qualities of the weapons themselves.

These considerations all make it important to pay full attention to factors of terrain and climate, the overall relationship of forces and the levels of training in assessing equipment performance. However, in addition to these general points concerning the danger of drawing too many lessons from a specific conflict, there are a number of peculiar features of the Falklands War that make it even more difficult to draw general conclusions. These features relate to both the geographical and political aspects of the war.

British forces are designed for use in the NATO area. Travel to the South Atlantic involved a long sea passage for which many items of equipment were unsuited. The damp conditions were harmful to systems depending on sensitive electronics. Cold conditions were also a feature of the Falklands, although preparations for combat in Norway meant that there were British units well able to cope. The long distances made all forms of communication difficult. The South Atlantic is not well covered by US communications or surveillance satellites.

Neither side was able to deploy a significant number of armoured vehicles on the islands. A lack of heavy-lift helicopters (UK forces had one: the others were lost on the *Atlantic Conveyor*) impeded mobility. This, plus the limited ability to apply air power to the land battle, meant that the land campaign bore scant resemblance to modern armoured warfare. Although both sides enjoyed some modern equipment, there were important gaps – for example a lack of electronic countermeasures (ECM).

Argentina had a number of geographical advantages but these were not fully exploited. In general this was a far less sophisticated enemy than would be faced in a central war. It would appear that the Argentine Government had not expected any British response and so both the timing of the initial invasion and the subsequent military occupation were not designed to take full military advantage of surprise. In attacking the British landing at Port San Carlos the Argentine Air Force made the fundamental error of attacking escorts rather than supply ships.

The war was fought without the close involvement of allies. Britain was fortunate in getting supplies of some key items of equipment from the United States but at no point could it leave important military tasks to an ally. This fact is very important when drawing lessons concerning the appropriate mix of forces. Large gaps that appeared when fighting alone could be swiftly closed when fighting alongside allies.

None the less, the degree of American help, especially after the 'tilt' of the end of April, did make a difference. The most important assistance was provided right from the start with the British use of Wideawake airfield on Ascension Island. The island itself was British property and a US refusal of the facilities would have had enormous repercussions, possibly affecting their own use of the more important American base on the British-owned island of Diego Garcia in the Indian Ocean. Another important contribution was in the re-fuelling effort for the task force. In terms of hardware, reports suggest supplies of Shrike anti-radar weapons, limpet mines, Stinger shoulder-fired anti-aircraft missiles, Harpoon air-launched anti-ship missiles and Sidewinder air-to-air missiles for the Harrier. The Sidewinders were supposed to replenish Britain's NATO stocks but some may have found their way to the South Atlantic. The Sidewinder–Harrier combination was one of the great success stories of the war. Similarly, the assignment of extra US KC135 tankers to NATO allowed the UK Victors to be released for Falklands duty. In addition, the US provided intelligence information, although not to the extent widely believed at the time. The most important intelligence tended to be signals traffic from Argentina and not satellite photography. In a war that can be described as a 'close run thing', Argentina can be forgiven for a suspicion that assistance at the margins might have made all the difference. The visibility of the assistance was costly for the United States in Latin American where this aid to an external power was used to berate it for its lack of sympathy for *real* American aspirations.

Another factor peculiar to this war was that it was limited in time, space, means and objectives. It was unlikely to turn into a long war of attrition and certainly not to 'go nuclear'. Either of these possibilities would have had a significant effect on the performance of systems.

The key differences between the two sides were in the

organization of their military forces and their professionalism. Argentine forces were riven by conflicts between officers and men, regulars and conscripts, which impaired their performance. At the end General Menendez did not even have an accurate picture of all the forces under his command. The British forces had the advantage in training, stamina and leadership and so demonstrated the virtues of military professionalism. In a war in which physical elements such as terrain and climate loomed as large as the technical factors, the traditional military virtues could be decisive. In this sense, the important lessons of the war were old ones that had been neglected in the fixation on technological prowess and weapon inventories. If differences in skill and tactical ingenuity do help account for the relative successes, then this makes it dangerous to assume that comparable results would be achieved elsewhere against different belligerents.

By and large what was suspected was confirmed. Submarines may be of little use for showing the flag or carrying supplies but they are lethal instruments. Surface ships are extremely vulnerable to dedicated air attacks. The British fleet lacked sufficient air cover and early warning, spent much of the time in a confined space, but still shot down many attacking aircraft, so its losses may not have been excessive. The Argentine Air Force, however, was neither particularly modern nor designed for anti-shipping purposes.

It is of note that in this apparently unmodern was rates of ammunition usage were higher than allowed for in NATO plans for war against the Soviet Union. The supply chain was able to deliver twice the amount of ammunition that would have been considered necessary on NATO assumptions.

The technical lessons are thus ambiguous and the revived traditional lessons may only be relevant if future wars are to be fought in such unmodern conditions. At the very least the experience serves as a corrective to notions of electronic battlefields where human qualities are redundant and everything can be explained by cybernetics.

Political lessons

The first political lesson concerns military management. By and large, the British 'war cabinet' resisted the temptation to indulge too greatly in long-distance battle management (unlike US administrations in some recent crises). None the less, the fact that modern communications make it seem feasible to exercise political control on events 8,000 miles away encouraged the politicians to take responsibility for military events about which they were only dimly aware. The speed of communications is a complicating factor in modern warfare, different only in kind from the complications that once resulted from the slow passage of information. Now more information arrives from more directions than can be effectively assimilated by any policy-maker trying to manage a major crisis, and the quality of the information does not necessarily match the speed of its transmission. One might have hoped that modern communications would reduce the uncertainties that bedevil crisis management. In fact, they can make them worse.

The impact of uncertainty was evident throughout the Falklands conflict. A whole series of factors, which could not have been anticipated beforehand, swayed the course of individual engagements and might even have affected the final result. A mistaken judgement about the feasibility of landing men on a glacier at the island of South Georgia almost led to a tragedy in the first stage of the British military operation. An Argentine aircraft anxious to reduce its weight so that its fuel would take it home, unloaded its spare bombs and – without knowing – almost caught a British submarine. Towards the end of the campaign, when the British land commanders were huddled together in conference, a shell landed not many yards away. Unreliable information, confusing communications, misapprehensions of the other side's capabilities and intentions – all these factors can be as responsible for defeat as poor equipment, training and command.

The Royal Navy was assigned overall command responsibility which it exercised from its headquarters at Northwood on the outskirts of London, transmitting orders to the commander of the task force. Operations on land were the responsibility of the senior Army officer. The decision-making was by and large successful but there were still misunderstandings between the two services: the Army did not always understand why naval gunfire support had to be withdrawn at crucial moments or key ships kept back when they might have been useful.

These tensions were also found in Whitehall, although the clear lines of command helped prevent inter-service rivalries becoming too serious. The central staff at the Ministry of Defence busied themselves with attending to requests from the commanders and considering the broad policy options and the rules of engagement. Relations between the Ministry of Defence, the Foreign Office, the intelligence agencies and the cabinet office were also generally good. The comparison with Pentagon–State Department–CIA–White House relations in US foreign policy crises, where rivalry, tension and loose coordination often appear to be the rule, is instructive. Three possible explanations for the differences are the fragmented nature of US government at the best of times, the dominance of the executive branch by political appointees rather than a professional civil service, and the dispersal of the main actors around Washington. In London the key ministries are all within walking distance of each other, and the responsible officials are career civil servants who have often worked with each other for many years under successive governments. In Britain the tradition is one of collective responsibility, which encourages putting the agreed position forward even when it has been hotly disputed. This makes it harder to divide a government against itself; on the other hand it also often makes it extremely different for outsiders (including Parliament) to find out what is going on and identify the range of policy options truly available to the government.

In London there were inevitable tensions between different ministries and different ministers at those points where their interests and responsibilities pulled in different directions. At no point, however, did this become dangerously divisive so as to put the efficient management of the operation at risk. Again, one of the reasons for this is that after the initial shock and the despatch of the task force the Government was not faced with any fundamental challenges to its policy of the sort that might emerge through complete diplomatic isolation or military disaster.

If Argentina had been more conciliatory at critical moments this could have thrown into relief underlying tensions within the war cabinet. At the Foreign Office, Francis Pym, who was never one of Mrs Thatcher's closest colleagues, accepted the need for a serious exploration of a diplomatic settlement. The fact that his aproach was serious probably helped shift the onus of blame for the failure of these efforts away from London. The Prime Minister was unhappy with some of the concessions Britain was required to make during the negotiations. After the double shock of the *Belgrano* and the *Sheffield* the Prime Minister was prepared to give more diplomatic ground, but this was within clear limits. It is not hard to imagine the arguments that could have developed if, in the face of another military setback, with public opinion and Parliament becoming more uneasy with the conduct of the war, the Foreign Secretary had argued for exceeding those limits while the Prime Minister remained resolved to carry on regardless. The US Secretary of State Alexander Haig recalled that during some of his early conversations with the war cabinet Pym murmured 'Maybe we should ask the Falklanders how they feel about a war'. He was heatedly challenged by Mrs Thatcher, who warned that aggressors will always try to intimidate those against whom they aggress. Haig comments:

Had I been Francis Pym, I would not have counted my chances of remaining in the cabinet as being very great if I persisted in suggesting to the prime minister that a retreat from her principles might be desirable.

The 'war cabinet' took the fundamental decisions on diplomacy and military action but offered no advice on how to implement those decisions. The contrast with Churchill during the Second World War is noteworthy. Churchill's constant desire to second-guess the professional military was generally considered to be one of the least helpful aspects of his premiership. In 1982 the political leadership was much more passive when it came to specifically military problems. Although some members of the war cabinet had military experience at a junior level, none had the background or the expertise seriously to challenge the military advice proffered. Furthermore, they were conscious that if they did insist on changing operations against military advice and something went badly wrong, then the political costs of the meddling would be dear – not to mention the potential human costs. With the Chief of Defence Staff, Admiral Lewin, acting as the sole channel of military advice, the war cabinet was less likely to be aware of divisions of opinion within the military, and with the headquarters at Northwood often assuming that the politicians would not want to be briefed on every operational detail, the war cabinet was not necessarily sufficiently well informed to challenge the military advice even if it wanted to.

In the event the system worked well enough. The military were grateful for the civilians' constancy of political purpose and for keeping off their backs. Admiral Lewin understood the political aspects of the war and was skilful in his relationships with politicians. In the early weeks of the conflict a variety of constraints on operations were accepted so as not to interfere with the diplomatic side of the effort, but these were gradually eased as the military dimension of the conflict grew in importance.

Once more, it is not hard to imagine how things could have been different. When there was political pressure to get a move on with military operations, as there was while supplies were being brought ashore after the landing at Port San Carlos, then the responsible officers were very irritated. (This irritation could be directed at pressure coming from either military or civilian sources in London if it seemed insensitive to local conditions.) In a conflict of this sort, with each military operation replete with potential political consequences, the civilian–military relationship could soon have turned sour – especially if there had been a succession of major military failures.

This experience with a relatively simple conflict throws into relief the likely problems with lines of command in a

NATO–Warsaw Pact crisis, which would involve the co-ordination of a variety of governments each with its own views on the conduct of the crisis, some with a proclivity to interfere with field decisions, in circumstances where the political stakes were of a completely different order and the battlefield situation was much more fraught.

Crisis diplomacy

In the Falklands campaign, both nations believed and expected that military action would gain its justification through diplomacy. Certainly at the start both believed that military actions were necessary to give weight to political demands. It was hoped that a convincing display of military force would put pressure on the opponent to make concessions. Yet, despite this shared belief, in the end the matter was decided by force of arms and without a negotiated settlement. Military power is not a simple instrument of diplomacy. Once invoked it transforms diplomacy, as compulsion takes over from compromise. Military means come to demand commensurate political ends. After Britain was forced to fight for the Falkland Islands, the sort of diplomatic solution that would have been embraced a few weeks earlier now turned out to be an insult to the men who had died. At the end of the war, Britain found itself with a political commitment to the islands that had been absent before.

Some of the most important diplomatic lessons might be learned by the United States. The conflict damaged American relations with both belligerents. Britain resented the tardiness of full US support for its effort to defeat aggression and the blatant opposition to Britain's long-term plans for the islands. Argentina on the other hand still smarts from the active help given to an enemy in war. In practical terms, 1982 saw Britain siding more naturally with its European partners in Atlantic disputes and the Prime Minister regularly expressing her disappointment in the United States. Argentina withdrew the Military Advisors acting in Honduras, Guatemala and El Salvador. Life in the OAS became a touch more difficult.

There are lessons here for the United States in handling conflicts between two friendly countries. The familiar point concerning the need for sensitive political intelligence might be emphasized; the need not to allow global fixation to affect the appreciation of regional relationships and the sense of vital interests of regional powers could also be stressed. To nip a crisis in the bud, it may be better to be one-sided from the start, especially if that one side is the side with which you will eventually be found. Allies expect to be the beneficiaries and not the targets of influence and the desire not to offend either side weakens diplomacy. Secretary Haig became a mediator rather than an arbitrator, a channel of communication rather than an agent for knocking heads together. If the United States is going to step in to settle disputes of this sort, it must not be afraid of using what leverage it has to achieve a satisfactory solution.

One question is whether the United States really had much leverage in this case. Neither participant was economically or militarily dependent enough to put the United States in a position to turn off the military action. The arms transfers, however, provided it with slight leverage. But simply terminating all sales to an area of conflict, apart from displaying a certain naïvety over the purposes of the original transactions, punishes the ally most dependent on the sales. Unless there is a good reason, failing to fulfil existing contracts will inevitably damage long-term relations with a country. Arms sales are thus difficult instruments for the fine tuning of crisis diplomacy. Policy as to what to supply to whom in a crisis depends on a judgement about who is most deserving of support. As it happened, in 1982 the US Government was forbidden by Congress to supply arms to Argentina because sales were linked to progress on human rights violations.

Where a major power finds two states friendly to it entering into combat with each other, it is often both difficult and unsatisfactory to choose between them simply by referring to national interests, or to opt out of any choice at all. The dilemma can be eased though, by referring to the norms of international law or the judgements of international institutions. When faced with this sort of dilemma, it makes sense to refer to a higher authority. Furthermore, to the extent that these conflicts do not have a marked East–West dimension, vetoes are unlikely to be used in the United Nations Security Council (the only veto used during the Falklands was by Britain and, in an astonishingly confused manner, by the United States in the cease-fire vote of 4 June).

If there is a tendency towards regional disorders that cut across East–West lines, the major powers will increasingly have to take one-sided positions on conflicts in which their interests are bound up in an even-handed manner. One way to avoid embarrassment in such situations is to hide behind the international community. In these circumstances the logic of power politics and of international order both point to the need to strengthen the rule of law and the role of the United Nations.

The logic of escalation

Diplomacy is not a clear-cut alternative to military action, for it often depends on the assessment of the likely winner of an eventual battle. If one side is continually requested to hold back, its diplomatic position may deteriorate along with its military options. For the party that does not have time on its side, it is necessary to keep the military initiative. Moreover, this initiative rarely allows for gradual escalation. In general, graduated response is an ideal that can rarely be achieved in practice. An overwhelmingly superior country can show flexibility and patience, meting out the military medicine in small doses to begin with and then building up to something more substantial, but this course is unlikely to commend itself to a country risking defeat. There is a military logic which such a country dare not ignore: this logic warns that military options cannot be maintained indefinitely and that some are highly perishable; that there are risks attached to tentative actions taken merely for demonstrative effect and that, confronting a capable enemy, there may be risks attached to doing nothing at all; that military campaigns rarely involve a simple build-up to some grand finale, but that the bloodiest and most difficult operations may be amongst the earliest; and that military action is unpredictable, so that what looks good in the plans can look awful in reality.

In the Falklands War the engagement with the greatest casualties – the sinking of the *General Belgrano* – came right at the start of the actual fighting. It was an important military victory for Britain, yet it turned into a political defeat because of the premium the international community put on the appearance of avoiding escalation. Any military action that is not self-evidently for defensive purposes, even if it is pre-emptive, becomes an outrage. Measures such as economic sanctions or blockades are deemed more acceptable than any military action which tends to lead to direct casualties. (Yet if sanctions or blockades are to succeed it can only be by causing immense distress to civilians – while if they fail, those involved will still have suffered lasting disruption and the international community is left with a smouldering problem.) Theere is thus considerable political discouragement for going on to the military offensive unless it is going to be reasonably bloodless.

The relevance of this for crisis management seems to be as follows. First, the concept of 'escalation', which is now an established part of thinking on crisis and war, is in practice misleading, for it creates unreal expectations as to the likely development of a conflict. Secondly, there can rarely be a neat proportionality between ends and means. Thirdly, there is a diplomatic as well as often a military advantage in forcing the enemy to initiate battle.

7 The Politics of Crisis

The Prime Minister, shortly after she came into office, received a soubriquet as the 'Iron Lady'. . . . there was no reason to suppose that the Right Hon. Lady did not welcome and, indeed, take pride in that description. In the next week or two this House, the nation and the Right Hon. Lady will learn of what metal she is made.
Enoch Powell MP, House of Commons, 3 April 1982

The human and material costs of war can be readily appreciated while the strategic logic and diplomatic manoeuvering may seem confusing and misguided. For these reasons democracies are not expected to be very effective when it comes to conducting wars fought for something other than national survival. Yet the War of the Falkland Islands showed that there is nothing inevitable about this. Since the American experience with Vietnam there has been an assumption that democratic societies have a low level of tolerance of war, with national will being sapped with each casualty and lurid media coverage. In the following chapter we will examine in detail the strength and character of popular support for the British Government during the campaign and its later impact on the Conservative Party's electoral fortunes. For the moment all we need to note is that the Government faced no difficulty in swinging public opinion behind it, despite its initial humiliation on 2 April, and support grew during the conflict. This support was also found in Parliament and the media and in a sense became mutually reinforcing.

Among the reasons for this are the natural tendency towards unity at moments of what are perceived to be national crisis, the decisiveness of the Government's response to the Argentine occupation, the widespread belief that Argentina was in the wrong and confidence in the effectivness of the policies adopted for dealing with the challenge. Any government may benefit from the 'rallying' effect of a major conflict, but for support to be sustained the quality of the Government's case and of its policies becomes increasingly important. One of the significant features of the conflict was the weakness of the domestic challenge to either the Government's objectives or methods.

To a large extent this was because Britain was never perceived to be in either diplomatic or military difficulties (even when it was). We have discussed in earlier chapters how Britain successfully ensured that it appeared as the aggrieved party in the United Nations, and that it was absolved for responsibility for the breakdown of the Haig mediation by the Secretary of State himself. Britain only began to lose the diplomatic initiative towards the end of the conflict when a military victory was already in sight. Similarly with the military initiative. Argentina seized the initiative to start with but failed to follow it through effectively. Thereafter it was Britain which set the terms of each stage of the conflict, improving its position each time. It is not hard to identify moments when successful Argentine action could have inflicted such costs on the task force that it might have been forced to withdraw, or when prudent preparations by the Argentine forces could have slowed down the British advance to the point where a stalemate would have had to be accepted. Time, as we have noted, was very much of the essence. As Mrs Thatcher remarked to the *Daily Express* after the conflict (26 July):

I had the winter at the back of my mind. *The winter*. What will the winter do? The wind, the cold. Down in South Georgia the ice, what will it do? It beat Napoleon at Moscow.

The question has already been asked many times in this book 'what would have happened in different circumstances?' What if Britain had not appeared to be keeping the initiative and the war had turned into a stalemate or even defeat; if allies had been more critical or indeed if Britain had been trying to fight in concert with them; if the fighting had not been so contained in time and space and so far away; if the issue had not been the simple one of aggression against British subjects by a military dictatorship but one much more complex and ambiguous, involving shadowy notions of national interest? Let us look at the areas from which potential opposition might have come.

Parliament and opposition

The war has been described as 'Parliament's War' because of the extraordinarily nationalistic debate that took place on the Saturday morning of 3 April. But in practice it was still the Government's war. The orders to prepare and despatch the task force had been delivered as soon as the Argentine occupation had become a certainty. Part of the atmosphere for the Parliamentary debate was created by the background of servicemen being recalled to their units, with notices to that effect appearing in main railway stations. The chief importance of the Parliamentary debate was that it set the tone for the domestic political debate on the conflict.

The very fact that Parliament was in session on a Saturday morning added to the sense of gravity. Speech after speech deplored the Argentine invasion and urged all necessary action be taken to recover the islands. The language was not that of calm moderation: for example, Conservative backbencher Bernard Braine

The time for weasel words has ended. I expect action from this Government; and I hope that we shall get it . . . The very thought that our people, 1,800 people of British blood and bone, could be left in the hands of such criminals is enough to make any normal Englishman's blood – and the blood of Scotsmen and Welshmen – boil too.

The important feature of the debate was that such language came from the Labour benches as well as the Conservative. The Labour leader Michael Foot gave what was believed to be one of his best Parliamentary performances. The message was unmistakable.

There is no question in the Falkland Islands of any colonial dependence or anything of the sort. It is a question of people who wish to be associated with this country and who have built their whole lives on the basis of association with this country. We have a moral duty, a political duty and every other kind of duty to ensure that is sustained. We are paramountly concerned . . . about what we can do to protect those who rightly and naturally look to us for protection. So far, they have been betrayed. The responsibility for that betrayal rests with the Government. The Government must now prove by deeds – they will never be able to do it by words – that they are not responsible for the betrayal and cannot be faced with that charge.

Initially the opposition parties saw an opportunity to embarrass the government for its 'loss' of the islands. This line of attack inevitably led the opposition to be associated with the cause of the islands' recapture. By and large Foot and his colleagues stressed in their rhetoric the international principle at stake and the fascistic nature of the Argentine regime, rather than questions of British pride or the territorial issue. As time went on they urged a greater role for the United Nations, sought confirmation of serious negotiating and worried about evidence of military action. But at no time were they prepared to distance themselves from the overall objective of the termination of the Argentine occupation, or the exploits of the task force. Having sanctioned the sending of the task force they were not in a strong position to insist that it must not be used when Argentina was still refusing to withdraw its forces from the islands.

The opposition found it difficult to second-guess the Government's handling of the war. They were not, of course, in receipt of all the relevant information. The Government offered private briefings by officials for opposition leaders, which were accepted by the leaders of the Liberal and Social Democratic Parties, but the Labour leadership feared that this would to some extent co-opt them.

There were some notable dissidents in the House of Commons, especially in the ranks of the Labour Party, but they were never in a position to lead a national movement against the war. A few brave souls spoke out against doing anything rash in the debate of 3 April. As the conflict developed more made their disquiet known. In the only Parliamentary vote on the Government's handling of the campaign during the conflict, after the failure of the UN mission and on the eve of the landing at Port San Carlos, a group of Labour MPs moved a dissident closure motion. It was defeated by a vote of 296 to 33. Two of those who voted against the Government were the Welsh Nationalist MPs; Plaid Cymru was the only party officially to oppose the British military effort. It is perhaps relevant that the arguments adduced by the motion's proposer, Mr Tam Dalyell, were as much related to the immediate risks faced by the task force as to the long-term need for a cooperative relationship with Argentina in the South Atlantic. 'I take no joy whatsoever in saying this - to warn of a military defeat of the first magnitude'. He saw analogies with Dieppe and Iwo Jima. He totted up the whole of the Argentine Army (only a small portion of it was actually available for fighting) and warned that they would be fighting a holy war.

Should we not therefore say, faced with the stark reality of a war with unforeseeable consequences on a continent where we are friendless, that we advocate withdrawal of the task force to home ports?

Dalyell, then a front-bench spokesman on Science, lost his job for his stand, as did Andrew Faulds, spokesman on Arts.

In practice, the considerable amount of opposition through-out the country to the military operation, especially during its earlier stages, was never fully mobilized. The Campaign for Nuclear Disarmament organized a demonstration that achieved only a modest attendance. Even the opponents of the war could not actually support the Argentine occupation, and were obliged to argue the case for alternative forms of pressure such as economic sanctions. Few were prepared to say that the loss of the islands should be accepted as a humiliation and diplomacy directed solely at ensuring that those islanders who wanted to leave were resettled on favourable terms.

The economic dimension

There were a number of reasons to expect that the economic dimension would loom large in the politics of the crisis.

Military operations overseas are expensive. Often they are backed up by economic sanctions which interfere with normal patterns of trade. They create political uncertainty. None of this tends to appeal to financial markets.

Public opposition might have been expected if large sums of money were being spent on overseas military adventures. Diplomatic or military setbacks might have led to a loss of confidence in sterling, a sudden outflow of funds, a need for outside help to prevent a precipitate collapse in the value of the pound. At worst there might have been no help; at best it would have come with political conditions attached, such as a more conciliatory approach in the search for a peaceful settlement. Memories of the conclusion of the Suez crisis, when the British were forced to abandon their plans because of American financial pressure, would have reinforced this concern with the economic dimension.

Yet the economic dimension never assumed importance throughout the campaign. If the crisis had been a year earlier, when the economic news had been unremittingly gloomy, then the Government's task might have been a lot harder. However, the campaign came against the backdrop of news of recovery, with industrial confidence beginning to return, public spending apparently under control and inflation and interest rates both expected to fall. Because Britain avoided diplomatic isolation, unlike with Suez, the risk of American opposition was never sufficient to impress the financial markets. In addition, the move away from an era of fixed exchange rates meant that the system could respond more sensitively to the political uncertainty. There was none of the political symbolism and international responsibilities that once attached to holding the value of sterling.

Shares and sterling both fell sharply just after the Argentine invasion but both picked up as confidence grew that there would be a satisfactory resolution of the conflict. When the UN talks finally failed in mid-May, so making it likely that Britain would feel obliged to try to land troops on the islands, there was a sharp drop in both the Financial Times index and the exchange rate. Again there was a quick recovery as nerve was regained, and this was reinforced by the successful landing.

The main result of the conflict appears to have been to delay the Stock Exchange's hitting new peaks (a bull market had been predicted for 1982) rather than actually to depress it. The stock market was more interested in the effects of the conflict on the Conservative Government's re-election prospects than any direct economic impact. Once it was reassured that the conflict was making the Conservatives more electable, the index began to rise.

The Government did not find it necessary to raise taxes to pay for the war. The immediate costs were met out of a £2.4 billion contingency reserve within the Public Sector Borrowing Requirement. Against the better judgement of the Treasury, the Ministry of Defence was able to gain an agreement that the extra costs incurred as a result of the Falklands campaign would not need to be met out of the Ministry's projected budget but would be held in a separate account. This arrangement will come to an end in 1990.

The actual costs were substantial but they were also spread out and so limited in their impact. They can be divided into three: the immediate costs of the fighting; the cost of replacing lost equipment and the replenishment of stores; and the costs of building up the garrison after the war.

The campaign itself, Operation Corporate, is now estimated to have cost about £1.5 billion. The cost of replacing lost equipment is put at £1,278 million. The largest single item in this figure is £641 million for four new Type 22 frigates to replace the four warships lost in the campaign. The cost of a new landing ship (logistics) to replace *Sir Galahad* is put at £69 million, and new aircraft account for another £116 million. Some two-thirds of these total replacement costs fell on the defence budget in the period ending April 1986. However, the final payments will not be made until 1990. In spreading out the costs the Government has spread the financial burden.

A similar pattern can be observed with the garrison costs. These will come to £1,777 million by 1990. Apart from the actual garrison running costs, which were close to £200 million per annum and are now closer to £100 million, the major items are airfield works (at £295 million) and new equipment (£280 million). About two-thirds of the total costs of the garrison had been met by April 1986. The total cost of the Falkland War therefore comes out at some £3.5 billion.

The media

If things had gone badly or the conflict had dragged on then of course the political debate would soon have changed. The speed and success of the Government's prosecution of the war can tell us little about the political consequences of a prolonged and messy conflict. However, there are some broad observations that can be made in terms of public support for overseas military operations. The first of these concerns the role of the media.

In general, the media supported the Government. Some newspapers fell over themselves in their efforts to demonstrate solidarity with the task force, describing the campaign in terms of great national fervour, although actually this does not appear to have made a great impression on the general population. The *Sun* was the most notable offender in this regard, with its headline 'Gotcha' after the sinking of the *Belgrano* becoming a particularly notorious example of bad taste. Both the BBC and ITN were at pains to maintain some sort of arm's length relationship with the Government, although the approach in reporting always reflected a 'British' perspective. The BBC incurred the Prime Minister's displeasure for some of its reporting and commentary, and in particular for one programme which allowed the critics of military action to ventilate their views.

The Ministry of Defence had not incorporated a role for the media into its strategic planning. There were no contingency plans available in this case and Government policy on the release of information showed great inconsistencies. Correspondents were only allowed to accompany the task force after an enormous fuss, and their accreditation papers were left over from the Suez Crisis of 1956. The Royal Navy had little experience in public relations of this sort and tended to distrust the media; the Army, with its experience of Northern Ireland, tended to develop a better working relationship. No means were found to transmit television pictures back or even, for some time, black-and-white stills. (The Parliamentary Defence Committee conducted its first post-war investigation on this matter.) Here again, this was a very unusual and old-fashioned war. From the British, but not the Argentine, side there were no television images. Contrary to media legend the reasons why it was not possible to send back television pictures were technical and not political. Whether it would have made much difference to popular support for the war if the realities of combat had been more vivid is doubtful. Those military officers who expressed anxiety over the possibility of broadcasts showing combat were often as much concerned for the effects this might have on the families of their men, and the consequent impact on service morale.

The correspondents accompanying the task force were utterly dependent on the military for their stories and their external communications. This made possible tight censorship. The consequent public demand for information in Britain was met by incessant speculation and commentary by retired military officers, often to the irritation of their colleagues still in uniform who felt that, even if they were not giving away important information, they were providing an insight into the workings of the British military mind. The major source of leaks would appear to have been the Parliamentary lobby, which picked up reports of comments made by ministers to backbenchers (often, but not always, of a reassuring kind).

Armed force and democratic societies

The second general observation we might make concerns the attitude towards the use of armed force in a democratic society. Such societies are not allergic to the use of military might. It is still widely accepted that there are things worth fighting for. There is no evidence that the good society and the welfare state have had a softening effect, as many commentators have supposed. Nor, despite the efforts of some sections of the press, was the public afflicted by a crude and belligerent nationalism that ignored the political context of the fight and the need for restraint in certain areas.

The conflict demonstrated that people are prepared to fight for goals related to the essence of nationhood; that is, in the face of a direct threat to British territory and British people and British values. An interesting question is whether the government and the task force would have commanded the same level of public support if the conflict had been over something not so directly British but with implications far more substantial for the security and well-being of the country. Suppose, for instance, the crisis had involved a direct threat to the Omani regime, which Britain has done much to sustain. Such a threat could be seen to effect the equilibrium of the Middle East in general and Saudi Arabia in particular, and thus continuity of Western oil supplies. This, after all, is the sort of contingency which many have argued should govern much of our defence planning. It is not clear whether there would have been a comparable response to activity that could not so readily be justified by reference to the symbols of sovereignty. The prominence given in 1987 to the role of British warships in protecting British shipping passing through the Gulf suggests a much more equivocal attitude towards this sort of intervention.

The conflict is also relevant to the debate on conscription. Some have assumed that the squeeze on available manpower resulting from long-term demographic trends combined with the need to keep up service numbers, and indeed to increase them to allow for a shift from nuclear to a conventional bias in NATO strategy, is creating a strong case for a return to conscription. Others support such a move as a means of improving relations between the services and the rest of society. It would seem, however, that the population generally looks benevolently enough on the armed services as they are presently constituted and the relationship is not antagonistic. We have also seen the efficiency that comes from having professional forces. The main point is that the general assessment of tolerable risk might have been very different if a substantial number of conscripts had been likely to suffer the consequences of miscalculation.

8 Public Opinion during the War

The lesson of the Falklands is that Britain has not changed and that this nation still has those sterling qualities which shine through our history
Prime Minister Margaret Thatcher, speech to
Conservative Party rally, 3 July 1982

There is a considerable amount of opinion poll material available from the period of the Falklands crisis, although in general it is always dangerous to attempt to draw too many conclusions from such surveys. However, the techniques used by the various polling organizations are now well developed, and while there is an unavoidable margin of error, so long as one is searching for trends or a broad feel for public attitudes this margin does not represent a great handicap. The problems with opinion poll surveys lie with the phrasing of questions and the assumptions that are often left unstated or unexplored in the time available to conduct an interview. The question may turn out to have been leading, or perhaps the respondent was given an inadequate range of responses from which to choose. As a result the answers may be contradictory, especially on subjects with a low public profile where the respondent may not have developed considered opinions. Again the polling organizations are aware of these problems and try to avoid systematic bias in the questions but there are limits to objectivity in these matters. Another failing may be that survey data will be incomplete and frustrating when critical questions have been either not asked or not repeated regularly so as to facilitate monitoring of changing attitudes over time.

Despite all these problems, however, when used with care opinion poll data can be extremely revealing and, in the absence of better indicators, are often all we have to go on when making judgements with regard to public opinion. In the case of the Falklands the great public interest in the campaign meant that the respondents in the many polls were likely to have informed and considered views on the various issues raised, compared with other less focused and less prominent defence and foreign affairs issues.

After an initial survey commissioned by *The Economist* in early April of more than 1,000 adults over 18, Market and Opinion Research International (MORI) returned regularly to 400–500 of the original respondents to monitor the changes in their views, often using the same questions. These interviews, of which there were six waves in all spanning the whole conflict, constitute a valuable set of data and provides the core of the analysis developed below. Other polling organizations were also active over this period and where possible their findings have been incorporated into the analysis.*

The quality of crisis management

The first poll was conducted by National Opinion Polls (NOP) after the announcement of the despatch of the task force and when Lord Carrington was in the process of resigning as Foreign Secretary. Only 12 per cent of respondents were prepared to absolve the Government of blame for the crisis; 58 per cent blamed it a lot and 22 per cent, a little. Gallup obtained a similar result a week later. While the later military successes clouded the memory of the first days of the crisis, a Gallup poll at the end of May still found 64 per cent of those polled believing that the Government had been caught off guard by the crisis.

The early NOP poll found that of those blaming the Government, particular blame was evenly divided between the Prime Minister (36 per cent), the Defence Secretary, John Nott (39 per cent), and the Foreign Secretary, Lord Carrington, who did resign (41 per cent). Not everyone agreed that resignations were required, but there was a clear preference that if resignations were in order then both Nott and Carrington should go

*Full details of the various polls are provided in Appendix Two

(45 per cent), with only 8 per cent arguing for Nott alone and 6 per cent for Carrington alone. The slightly higher figure for Nott may reflect the bad press he received after his Parliamentary performance on 3 April. The first MORI poll of mid-April still found opinion divided on the resignation of Carrington and the desirability of Nott's resignation. Of those polled, 34 per cent considered that the Prime Minister should have resigned.

The negative early reactions illuminated by the NOP poll were reflected in 50 per cent support for the view that the crisis had worsened Britain's standing in the world. The message for the Government was underlined by a question being put to professed Conservative voters. If the Government failed to regain the islands would they still vote the same way? Fifteen per cent said they would be less likely to do so.

What seems to have saved the Government was the decisive action it took immediately to isolate Argentina diplomatically and economically and to send the task force. The first MORI poll on 14 April found 60 per cent of the respondents happy with the Government's handling of the crisis and only 30 per cent dissatisfied. When considering the future of the conflict, 20 per cent thought Argentina would give up the Falklands without a fight. Another 50 per cent divided evenly between those who thought it would be sufficient to fight a naval battle and those who expected that British troops would need to be landed if the islands were to be retaken. Of the others, 16 per cent expected that in the end Britain would have to lease the Islands back from Argentina; only 6 per cent thought that Britain would eventually have to back down.

From the start 83 per cent of the panel said they cared personally that Britain should regain the Falklands, although this included 32 per cent who cared 'only a little'. This percentage was remarkably constant throughout the conflict. What did change was the saliency of the issue. In early April some 39 per cent of the panel thought the Falklands was the most important issue facing the country, exactly the same percentage as chose unemployment (the previous month unemployment had dominated the political debate with 63 per cent identifying it as the most important issue). By early May, the fourth wave of the MORI panel saw the Falklands as by far the most important (61 per cent) with unemployment now well behind (25 per cent).

Satisfaction with the Government's handling of the crisis grew as it developed. In the *Economist* panel, the satisfaction ratings reached 68 per cent in the second set of interviews and 76 per cent by the third set at the end of April. By the end of the conflict, with the islands regained, this figure had reached 84 per cent. The only wobble came in early May. Interviews conducted after the sinking of the *Belgrano* and over the period when the *Sheffield* was lost show a decline in the satisfaction rating from 76 per cent to 71 per cent. This was the point in the conflict when the Government itself actually came closest to losing its nerve.

From the start there was an overwhelming majority supporting the sending of the task force, again at around the 80 per cent level (83–85 per cent in the MORI polls), and this at least in the earlier stages of the conflict ran consistently ahead of the approval of the Government's handling of the crisis. This was in part because there was a substantial minority in favour of tougher action than the Government was taking. For example, a Gallup poll of 9–13 April found 78 per cent approving the sending of the task force with 16 per cent against and 6 per cent 'don't knows', as against figures of 67 per cent, 24 per cent and 9 per cent respectively for the Government's actions in general. Those approving the Government's action had a mixture of motives of which the two most popular were that the Falkland Islands were a British colony (23 per cent) and that the nation's international image was at stake (16 per cent). Of 24 per cent disapproving of the Government's actions, 5 per cent did so because of the original Government mistake in allowing the crisis to develop and 6 per cent (a quarter of this category) because the Government had been slow off the mark. Only 3 per cent felt that Argentina should be allowed the islands and 2 per cent gave as their reason the fear of bloodshed. Almost a month later, when there was considerable concern over the sinkings of the *Belgrano* and the *Sheffield*, Gallup found that while 51 per cent felt that the Government position in the negotiations was about right, far more (27 per cent) felt it was not being tough enough than felt it was being too tough (17 per cent).

The methods of crisis management

One of the most interesting aspects of the opinion poll data is the insight they provide into the public understanding of the forms of pressure appropriate to such a crisis and the impact of critical events in the conflict on this understanding. From the start NOP found that 56 per cent were prepared for the islands to be regained by force, with 46 per cent preferring that this be achieved by diplomacy. A week into the crisis Gallup found a strong majority (86 per cent to 9 per cent against) for cutting off all trade with Argentina, a clear majority for attacking Argentine ships and landing British troops on the islands (61 per cent to 32 per cent) and a significant minority (24 per cent to 68 per cent) prepared to attack the Argentine mainland.

From the start MORI canvassed its panel with a range of options in addition to the sending of the task force. The first set of interviews showed strong support for the non-violent forms of pressure – the banning of Argentine imports (84 per cent) and freezing of Argentine assets in British banks (82 per cent). Interestingly, there was a smaller majority in favour of severing diplomatic relations (71 per cent for; 22 per cent against), perhaps reflecting recognition of the need for an eventual diplomatic settlement. In terms of a negotiated solution, the greatest preference was for allowing the United Nations to take over the administration of the islands. This was supported by a slight majority in the first set of interviews (45 per cent for; 42 per cent against) and then lost favour in the weeks prior to the actual fighting. It was opposed by 50 per cent of the panel, as against 40 per cent for, just before the main fighting began. After the start of hostilities it regained favour and was supported by 51 per cent by the end of May. By contrast, the option that had seemed most promising to the Foreign Office in the years preceding the crisis – the islands' becoming Argentine territory but then being leased back to the British Government for administration – never had more than 26 per cent of the panel's support and this declined steadily with the conflict.

On the military options, the two most likely gained moderate support: 52 per cent (with 39 per cent against) were prepared to see Argentine ships sunk, while 67 per cent (24 per cent against) were prepared to land troops on the islands. Support for landing troops declined marginally to 65 per cent in the next two sets of interviews of the panel, only picking up as the problems of a continuing confrontation at sea became apparent. However, in a separate poll conducted for the *Daily Star* in late April, MORI found 78 per cent agreeing that the armed forces should attempt to regain sovereignty by invading the islands.

The resistance to the sinking of ships is noteworthy. It is not wholly consistent with the willingness of 80 per cent of the panel to impose a blockade of the islands. Up to the point where ships actually began to get sunk, the readiness to take this step grew steadily. After ships had been sunk, however, including a number of British ships, resistance to further action of this sort had declined dramatically. By the fifth set of MORI interviews, after the San Carlos landings, 79 per cent supported the sinking of ships.

We have already noted the substantial minority – around a quarter of those polled – who were prepared to take extremely strong action against Argentina. In the first MORI poll 28 per cent were prepared to bomb Argentine Air and Naval bases (63 per cent against) and 21 per cent were prepared to invade the Argentine mainland (73 per cent against). Astonishingly, 5 per cent were ready to use nuclear weapons against Argentina, with 93 per cent opposed to such a step and another 2 per cent apparently finding it difficult to make up their minds on this matter. In line with the hawkish sentiment, 24 per cent were prepared to tolerate the internment of Argentine citizens in Britain (68 per cent against). Most of these options were not followed up in the subsequent re-interviewing. The exception was the bombing of Argentine bases, for which support grew marginally prior to hostilities and then significantly thereafter, possibly because British ships were being attacked by aircraft from these bases. By late May 47 per cent of the panel would have supported attacks on the bases, although this would still have been opposed by 49 per cent.

Although as Britain took stronger military action the proportion of those who considered that British action was too weak declined, Gallup surveys found that well over a third of those polled believed until the end of the conflict that an invasion of the Islands should have been undertaken earlier. In mid-May 12 per cent were prepared to support an invasion of Argentina. This went down to 9 per cent in early June, perhaps only because by this time there was even less of a military case for such an operation.

The proportion generally more doveish than the Government also tended towards a quarter of the electorate. Thus in the same Gallup polls, some 23 per cent in mid-May were urging that more effort be put into the negotiations, and this rose to 26 per cent by early June – by which time the Government was hardly even going through the motions of seeking a diplomatic settlement.

It is of interest that in the MORI panel there was two-thirds support for pressing ahead with military force even in the face of opposition from the United States, up to the point where it was clear that this was not going to be an issue. For those with memories of Suez, this was significant.

Support for the landing of troops grew in a similar manner. At the time of the recapture of South Georgia and just before Secretary of State Haig's efforts at mediation broke down, 43 per cent of the MORI panel in the third set of interviews agreed that Britain should be prepared to fire the first shot even if diplomatic talks were still taking place. The failure of the mediation presumably made it easier for the 51 per cent who opposed this view to accept the need for military action.

By the start of May, with military action now under way, the number of those in the MORI panel who felt that the Government was not being tough enough had declined to 7 per cent. A clear 64 per cent felt that the Government's use of force was about right while now 25 per cent were concerned that the Government was too willing to use force. The sinking of the *General Belgrano* would appear to have influenced this judgement. While a clear 81 per cent (14 per cent against) approved the bombing of the Stanley airport on 1 May, only 46 per cent, with a notable 44 per cent against, approved the sinking of the *Belgrano*.

The MORI panel also suggested that while support for the task force was widely and evenly spread across all ages and social groups, women were notably less prepared to sanction military action, and along with younger people were generally prepared to be more conciliatory in the negotiations. Men supported attacks on Argentine ships by two to one, while women were marginally opposed.

The costs of crisis management

With regard to the difficult question of what it was worth to regain sovereignty over the islands, the MORI panel produced some interesting findings. Most marked was the willingness to accept increased costs as the conflict developed. The question of whether something is worth a speculative, prospective cost is quite different from whether, after an initial and unwelcome investment in lives and resources, that objective should be renounced. The panel were asked to evaluate the option of taking the Falklands against three sets of costs: loss of British servicemen's lives, loss of Falkland Islanders' lives and increased taxes to meet the cost of military and naval forces. Apart from one point on the eve of hostilities when opinion was equally divided, there was never a majority in the panel tolerating the loss of Falkland Islanders' lives, although the majority opposed narrowed from 55 for to 36 per cent against at the start of the conflict to 48 to 45 per cent a month later. At the start of the conflict there was also a majority opposing the loss of servicemen's lives (49 per cent for to 44 per cent against), but on the eve of the conflict there was a substantial majority in favour (58 to 37 per cent), declining slightly as the first lives were lost (53 to 43 per cent) and then picking up well into the campaign (62 to 34 per cent). After the fighting was over some 76 per cent felt that the retention of the islands had been worth the loss of lives, with only 22 per cent against. As far as increased taxes went, there was always a majority in favour if it was necessary to regain and then protect the islands. In the first set of interviews 58 per cent supported this, with 36 per cent against. By the end of the conflict however 71 per cent were now prepared to pay extra taxes to prevent a recurrence. As many as 46 per cent were prepared to see a reduction in NATO commitments to defend the islands.

At the start of the conflict NOP found that the majority (56 per cent) was in favour of holding on to the islands indefinitely should they be recaptured, with just over a third still prepared to negotiate. Similar proportions were found in the MORI panel right at the end of the conflict when asked if it would be wrong to have fought the war if the Government intended to give up the Islands in the long run. Gallup found that some 22 per cent of those polled expected that the islands would be given to Argentina in the long term. The MORI panel found consistently high support for the proposition in any negotiations that the islanders should have the final say over the issue of sovereignty (peaking at 83 per cent in late May but declining to 72 per cent by the end of the conflict). This was the basis of the dispute with Argentina from early on. However, it is interesting that when MORI, in a poll conducted for the *Sunday Times*, asked whether long-term policy on the Falkland Islands should be determined by the wishes of the islanders alone, or by the interests of Britain as a whole taking the islanders' views into account, the overwhelming majority supported the latter (72 per cent as against 24 per cent). The limits to self-determination were understood.

The consequences of crisis management

The long-term political impact of the crisis has become a matter of some dispute. In the aftermath of the 1983 general election it was widely believed that the 'Falklands factor' had been the key to the Conservative Party's re-election. Prior to the war dissatisfaction with Mrs Thatcher's administration had been running high. By the end of the conflict it enjoyed substantial popular support and it never again trailed in the polls. However, a team from the University of Essex, argued in an article published in the summer of 1987 that the Falklands factor has been exaggerated and that it was macroeconomic management rather than crisis management which was responsible for a turnaround in the Government's fortunes: 'The Falklands crisis merely coincided with a jump in government popularity which would have occurred anyway in the wake of Geoffrey Howe's 1982 budget.'*

The evidence for this in terms of the June 1983 election is impressive and is based on an extraordinarily sophisticated analysis of the relationship between economic trends and voter preferences. The first two years of the Thatcher Government had been extremely difficult economically and this affected voters' views of their personal prospects, which soon translated into support for opposition parties. During 1981 the main beneficiaries of this concern had been the newly formed Social Democratic Party, led by former Labour cabinet ministers and then moving into tentative alliance with the Liberal Party.

In March 1982 the Chancellor's fourth budget had been more relaxed than the previous three. The economic indicators began to suggest that the country was moving out of the recession and so individuals were able to be more positive about their personal prospects. Incomes and consumer spending began to rise and interest rates fall.

There seems little reason to question that in June 1983, a year after the close of the conflict, the performance of the economy was of greater importance than any other issue when the electorate made up its mind on how to vote. In the election campaign itself the future of the Falklands was not pressed as a major issue. The Labour Party had decided to refrain from drawing attention to the matter but then was let down by remarks made by Denis Healey (who described the Prime Minister as 'glorifying in slaughter') and Neil Kinnock (who spoke of people leaving their 'guts' at 'Goose Green'). In general, if the Falklands factor was influencing voters it was because of their memories of a year earlier rather than the campaign itself.

*David Sanders et al., 'Government popularity and the Falklands War: a reassessment', *British Journal of Political Science*, 17 (1987), pp. 281–313.

It is also clear from the poll evidence that the Conservative Party was recovering in the opinion polls prior to the Argentine occupation of the islands. The recovery pre-dates the March 1982 budget and the economic upswing. It can largely be traced to the decline in the rating of the SDP–Liberal alliance from November 1981 after the first rush of enthusiasm. With the Labour Party still divided, it seems plausible that an economic recovery of the sort that did begin around this time would have been sufficient to see the Government through the next general election even without the Falklands effect.

The Essex team however may have been too dismissive of the immediate impact of the Falklands War on the Conservative Party's fortunes. At the start of the conflict MORI found the Alliance slightly ahead in the polls at 34 per cent with the Conservatives just below at 33 and Labour at 31. Two weeks into the conflict it was still a three-horse race, except that the Alliance were now third and the Conservatives had edged into the lead. By the end of April the Conservatives had a clear lead and by the end of May had dramatically improved their position to 51 per cent of the vote, with Labour now at 25 per cent and the Alliance at 22. At the end of the conflict in mid-June the Conservatives still held this support, while Labour had improved to 29 per cent at the expense of the Alliance now on 17. Other polls over this period varied in their details but the overall trends were the same. Although there was a falling off of Conservative Party support in subsequent months, the Government never looked to be in serious difficulty thereafter.

The Essex team argues that this dramatic rise in Conservative popularity would have been predicted on their model because of the rise of personal expectations by electors over these months irrespective of the Falklands issue. At most, they suggest that the Falklands effect was extremely small (in the region of 3 per cent) above the expected rise in Conservative popularity and highly ephemeral, lasting three months at most.

It is impossible to prove or disprove such an analysis. However, two points can be made. First, whatever voters might have thought in the absence of the conflict, it made a difference to the reasons given for favouring the Government during these months. From 21 to 26 April and then from 28 April to 5 May voters were asked by Gallup if anything had happened during the previous week to make them feel more or less favourably inclined towards the Government. In the first poll 40 per cent felt more favourable, 15 per cent less so and 45 per cent were as before; in the second poll, 36 per cent felt more favourable, 18 per cent less so and 46 per cent no different. When those who had changed their views were asked why, the overwhelming majority – both more and less favourable – cited the Falklands. The figures were 94 and 92 per cent respectively for the more favourable, 89 and 93 per cent for less favourable. There seems little doubt that over this period the Falklands was dominating individual judgements on political preferences.

In subsequent polls through May and June Gallup asked voters whether a variety of items had made respondents feel more or less favourably inclined towards the Government. With the exception of Mrs Thatcher herself, whose positive impact exceeded the negative by a thin majority of 36 to 34 per cent, all the factors other than the Falklands recorded consistently against the Government. This included the key economic indicators which on the Essex model might have been expected to show for the Government over this period. Thus the Government's taxation policy made 14 per cent feel more favourable in late May and 17 per cent in mid-June. It made 43 and 46 per cent respectively feel less favourable. Similarly with the cost of living: it made 14 and 13 per cent respectively think more favourably, and 53 and 59 per cent think less favourably. For unemployment (consistently cited during this period in other polls as one of the most important issues facing the country) the Government's position was even worse. Around 70 per cent said unemployment made them think less favourably while only a few per cent said it made them think more favourably.

The impact on views of the Labour Party was also evident. As the image of the Party declined during April to June 1982, the Falklands was cited as a factor in late April by some 78 per cent of those who now thought less well of the Party. The impact of this factor declined steadily over the next few months, but popular views on the Labour Party were still not governed by the quality of its economic policies but by the quality of the leadership provided by Michael Foot and the challenge to it posed by Tony Benn.

It may be that the Falklands crowded out consideration of all other issues, including the pick up in economic indicators. There does not seem to be any evidence that without the Falklands the Government would have seen a surge in support at that time. More likely is that the surge in Conservative support came earlier than it would have done without the Falklands. This had important implications for the morale of all the political parties and also perhaps for the confidence in overall Government policies, including those on the economy. It is also relevant that the strengthening of the economy over this period greatly facilitated crisis management. If the economy had been weak then international financial sentiment might have told against the despatch of the task force and the prosecution of the war.

The second point is that the important counter-factual may not be what would have happened if the Falklands conflict had not occurred, but if the military campaign had ended in disaster or if there had simply been no military option available to the Government in April 1982. The fact that the Government was able to send a task force of the necessary strength as quickly as it did, so that it could arrive in time to make an impact before poor weather made the operation even more difficult, was extremely fortuitous. If the Junta had waited a couple of months, the British military position would have been far worse and even hopeless. As it was, the Government was taking a gamble with the task force. The speed with which the Government acted in early April appears to have headed off a major crisis of confidence over the dismal handling of the events leading up the occupation. If the Government had failed to respond decisively to the Argentine invasion or had responded decisively but disastrously, then strength in the economy might not have been sufficient to save the Conservative Government.

9 Was It Worth It?

We went to fight because they had invaded British territory. And it's really all a question of pride. I think Britain had to have that pride in herself or as a nation, we would have just been what now? They had to do it. Ah . . . the price my family paid. No one will ever know . . . exactly what price we paid.
Perhaps it was worth it for Britain's sake.
Dorothy Foulkes, *The Falklands War — The Untold Story*, Yorkshire Television, April 1987

This observation on the Falklands campaign comes not from one of those commanding it from a grand strategic height, but from someone caught up in it, a woman widowed by the war. It suggests a tension between anger that her husband had died for something as intangible as national pride, and a sort of consolation that a nation's pride might be just about worth dying for.

In this concluding chapter we will examine the rights and wrongs of the Falklands conflict. The issue involves questions both of morality – were these circumstances where the use of armed force was justified? – and of prudence – were the assets at stake worth the human and material costs of retrieving them? These questions of value often appear to turn on questions of fact. In assessing the judgements of the time, however, we must remember that much of what we know now with hindsight was then only a matter of speculation.

The origins of any major conflict are normally complex and this makes the assignment of blame, often a matter of critical political importance, rarely straightforward. The conduct of war brings out the best and worst in both nations and individuals. It is unusual for either to take a war through to its conclusion in a morally blameless fashion. Success in war can depend on cool nerves, heroism and resolve, which appear admirable, but may also involve ruthlessness and a capacity for deception. It can bring to the fore a warm communal spirit, but one forged through chauvinism and triumphalism.

Most of all war involves organized killing, putting young men in positions of extreme danger, where they can often only survive by killing and maiming other young men. The Falklands War was by no means bloody by twentieth-century standards, or even by the standards of other conflicts under way at the same time – in the Lebanon, Afghanistan, Iran–Iraq and Kampuchea – but it was bloody enough for those involved.

Because war involves organized killing, it has always been held, at least in the moral traditions of the West, to require special justification. This is not simply a question of ethics unrelated to and, therefore, disregarded in the 'real world' of political life. Political leaders rarely offer cynical explanations for their politics and behaviour, but instead seek to develop them through forms of moral reasoning. They appeal to values which they believe to be shared by the community. On occasions they are obliged to modify their policy on discovering that their appeals are gaining no response, or that there are other values which are held more widely and more strongly.

It is a critical political skill to be able to develop policies in line with the moral sensibilities of the community. This is not to exaggerate popular high-mindedness, although few like to count themselves or their country as being wholly amoral. Rather it is to recognize that the considerable costs of war, economic as well as human, must be justified if they are to be tolerated. This task becomes even more important in a limited war, where national survival itself is not at stake.

Episodes such as the Falklands War provide us with an insight into the nature of the moral sensibilities of a country like Britain at a time of crisis. We noted in the previous chapter that there was a substantial political consensus in favour of the resort to armed force by the Government, and that the substantial minority dissenting lacked effective political leadership. We also saw how what seemed unacceptable during the early days of the crisis became tolerable as the conflict developed. Views concerning the proper rules by which to conduct wars can be amended as the other side is seen to be playing by different rules.

But while the moral parameters were fluid, they were never

absent, and politicians throughout attempted to shape the terms of the moral debate and remain sensitive to its nuances. There was worry and discomfort (perhaps sometimes marked by exaggerated and strident attempts at justification) when it seemed as if Britain was widely viewed within the international community as being in the wrong, such as with the sinking of the *Belgrano* or when vetoing attempts at the United Nations to get a cease-fire.

Granting that British policy-makers considered themselves to be operating within a framework of values, it might still be objected that this framework was deficient in key respects. In making up our own minds about the rights and wrongs of the affair we need to consider whether we share the same set of moral criteria, in which case at issue is the quality of their application in particular instances, or whether we prefer alternative criteria, in which case there is a conflict of values. However, in developing a moral critique of political leaders it is perhaps unreasonable to judge them according to moral traditions that have no strong roots in the community or are at variance with the views that they have espoused in the past.

However even a familiar and apparently popular set of values can not necessarily be forged into a single moral code to provide consistent guidance for political leaders at times of crisis. The values themselves are often in conflict, and there will be a natural tendency to accord greater weight to those which would be the most convenient or simple to follow. It may only be possible to work out their relevance in particular circumstances by reference to information that is not available and possible outcomes that cannot be predicted. Thus while political leaders may attempt to operate within some sort of moral framework this framework may not be very satisfactory and the uncertainty and confusion of the situation may make it difficult to follow.

The most important moral tradition in this area – the 'just war' tradition – survives largely because it is a check-list of factors rather than a means of resolving the dilemmas caused by conflicts of values. This traditional approach can be traced back to St Augustine. It provides a set of criteria that should be met if a war is to be considered just and another set that must be met if it is to be considered to have been fought in a just manner. According to this tradition the resort to force can only be justified if it is taken by those with legitimate authority, in response to a severe injustice, as a last resort when all other means have failed, and with the sole intention of righting the wrong and concluding the hostilties as soon as possible. There should be a likelihood of success and proportionality in that the evil resulting from the war should not be greater than the evil prevented or redressed. The conduct of war must be on the basis of discrimination between combatants and non-combatants and the continual application of the principle of proportionality.

This tradition is still accorded great respect and is very much in evidence in discussions on the morality of nuclear strategy. Its utility is limited by the fact that as few wars ever fully satisfy all criteria one must either assume war is always immoral (in which case why bother with the exercise) or assign a hierarchy to the various criteria. But the tradition provides no satisfactory means of doing this.

Another failing is that the criteria are easier to apply in retrospect than in prospect because the consequences of a war are extremely difficult to predict at the outset, and a war may be entered into with the best of motives but on the most erroneous of assumptions. Lastly, it treats the questions of going to war and the conduct of war as separate, and so fails to do justice to the substantial strategic decisions that must be taken during the course of a war, or to the link between the outcome of a war, upon which it must be judged, and its actual conduct.

The most important impact of the 'just war' tradition is the sense that there ought to be some proportionality between the ends and the means; whatever good is achieved by fighting a war must not be overwhelmed by the evil that will also result. As death and destruction are evil, and as a considerable amount of both can be produced in a war, the reasons for entering into one need therefore to be extremely good. In this light, let us look now at the British Government's case for entering into war over the Falklands issue.

The Government's case

The strongest version of the British Government's case (and in some aspects stronger than the Government might have made it) is as follows:

1 The Falkland Islands and its dependencies are sovereign British territory. Although the international community recognized a dispute over sovereignty, until the parties to the dispute formally altered the islands' status they were under British jurisdiction.
2 The islanders themselves were happy with the status quo and wanted it to continue. The repressive nature of recent Argentine regimes did not encourage a transfer of loyalties from London to Buenos Aires.
3 The islands themselves are strategically placed and, when the waters around them are included, they have substantial mineral resources. They also help establish Britain's position in Antarctica.
4 The seizure of the islands at the start of April 1982 was a blatant breach of international law, which stresses the need for the peaceful resolution of international disputes and condemns unprovoked aggression. The international community, with the exception of most Latin American states and to some extent the Eastern bloc, accepted that Britain was the aggrieved party. Many countries imposed economic sanctions against Argentina. Britain justified its actions throughout on the basis of not only UN Resolution 502, which required withdrawal of forces, but also Article 51 of the UN Charter which recognizes the 'inherent right to self-defence'.
5 Britain adopted all reasonable methods to retrieve the islands – political isolation, economic sanctions, diplomatic mediation as well as military force. Unfortunately only military force was capable of resolving the dispute, at least in such a way as to avoid rewarding Argentina for its original aggression.

6 The successful conduct of the war enhanced Britain's international standing and served as a reassurance to allies who might require Britain to act in a similar fashion on their behalf.

It is important to note that these arguments are *not* inter-dependent. Working backwards, (point 6) is a question of consequences, which at best refers to a useful spin-off, while (5) is a question of means and raises questions with regard to the efficacy of alternative forms of pressure in this particular set of circumstances. It is possible to accept that Britain was correct to oppose the Argentine occupation, but that the means chosen were wholly inappropriate, given the costs. Point (4) is also about means, but goes beyond their efficacy to relate particular means of resolving disputes to the requirements of the inter-national system as a whole. It is possible to applaud Britain for upholding international norms without accepting its underly-ing position on the Falklands.

The case assessed

Thus effective criticism of some aspects of the Government's case does not mean that all must fall. Points (1) and (2) can at least be qualified through the evident ambiguity in Britain's position prior to April 1982. As we noted in chapter 2, Britain's claim is by no means watertight and researchers such as Peter Beck of Kingston Polytechnic have found Foreign Office documents from earlier decades questioning the strength of the British claim. The British willingness to discuss sovereignty in negotiations since 1968 hardly suggests certainty on this matter. The unwillingness to accord the Falkland Islanders the full rights of British citizens in the 1981 Nationalities Act underlines this point. The Foreign Office would have been content with a 'lease-back' agreement with Argentina whereby sovereignty would have been conceded while guaranteeing in some way a British administration and way of life for the islanders.

The counter to these points might be that the quality of the Argentine case on sovereignty was not strong either, but it was backed by strong passions and a certain economic and geo-political logic. Its legal claims were dubious and the attempts by Buenos Aires to present the question as one of colonialism was specious. The local population was of British origin (admittedly in part because Argentine settlement had been prevented) and had no desire to be liberated.

Moving on to point (2), there is no doubt that the islanders themselves preferred the constitutional status quo. However, the principle of self-determination has not been treated as an absolute in the past. The desires of individuals, small communities or even quite substantial communities have been sacrificed in the past in the name of what has taken to be some greater cause. The inhabitants of the Indian Ocean island of Diego Garcia for example were moved to allow the island to develop as a military base. Successive British governments have refused to spend anything other than minimal amounts on the Falkland Islands and have clearly seen their economic viability as being dependent on forging links with the Latin American mainland, including Argentina. The population had declined to 1,800. Few declining communities of 1,800 could expect to exercise a virtual veto on official British policy when it came to defending their own interests.

Yet, having said all that, the fact that the principle of self-determination has been compromised in one set of circumstances does not provide a reason for disregarding it entirely in *all* circumstances. Furthermore, while pure self-determination is always an illusion, occupation by a foreign power is normally recognized to constitute the most direct challenge to this principle.

On these first two points, the British Government's motives have also been questioned. Britain has been fully prepared to deal with right-wing military regimes when it has suited its purposes, and in fact had close dealings with Chile, ruled by a regime at least as unsavoury as the Argentine Junta, throughout the Falklands conflict.

The argument that the Falkland Islands represent an important economic and strategic asset is at best unproved. If there are substantial mineral resources it would be difficult to exploit them without Argentine cooperation. In strategic terms, the Falklands had been seen to be a useful base but only in the days before the Panama Canal when critical sea routes passed by the islands. Recurrent interest in a South Atlantic Treaty Organization, to mirror NATO, has been shown to varying degrees by the major Latin American powers (Argentina, Chile, Brazil) and South Africa. But the South Atlantic is not central to the East–West conflict and the combinations required to forge a SATO fly in the face of political reality. Whatever the future potential, the resources devoted to this part of the world by successive British Governments up to 1982 indicate severe doubts over the value of the islands as an asset in themselves worthy of investment.

A regular charge has been made that the conflict was seized upon by the Royal Navy as a means of reversing the 1981 Defence Review and by the Government of Margaret Thatcher as a means of restoring a flagging popularity. Certainly the conflict did wonders for the popularity of the Conservative Party (although the divisions in the opposition camp and the revival of the economy were possibly eventually of greater importance) and the Royal Navy clawed back some of the ground lost in 1981. However, in both cases this was an enormous gamble which could have failed disastrously. The initial political humiliation of the loss of the Falklands would have been compounded had the task force suffered a military humiliation. If there was an opportunity that could be turned to domestic political advantage it was because it was presented by Argentina, which the British Government neither invited nor welcomed.

These criticisms of Government policy are not all invalid in themselves. They help expose flaws in the handling of policy with regard to the Falklands Islands up to 1982 and the mixture of motives and principles with which policy was forged as the crisis developed. But they do not undermine the central feature of the case in favour of intervention, which is found in point (4) above.

It could be argued, after all, that in 1939 the British Government had shown itself perfectly prepared to deal with dictatorships. After the Second World War the Conservative Party attempted (albeit with a complete lack of success) to turn the successful outcome to its electoral advantage. Although invasion of Poland triggered the declaration of war against Germany, Britain could do little in the immediate circumstances of September 1939 to help Poland repel German occupation. Chamberlain could have said, as he had said about Czechoslovakia the previous year, that this was 'a faraway country of which we know little'. What made the situation different in September 1939 was that Hitler was showing such disregard for the norms of international behaviour, making it necessary to take decisive action to restore those norms.

Thus while the fate of the islanders was clearly relevant, what was at stake in 1982 was the overall conduct of international affairs. It would not have been worth going to war over 'that ice-cold bunch of land', as President Reagan described the islands. Many of those engaged in the fighting were dismayed over the amount of effort that went into recovering territory so sparsely inhabited and of such little economic interest – more a liability than an asset. Some sought evidence that there might be mineral wealth yet to be tapped. Others took comfort from the gratitude shown by the islanders at their liberation. The most important justification, however, was to thwart an attempt to resolve by force of arms a dispute that was subject to negotiation.

So it is possible to criticize the Government's handling of the Falklands issue prior to 1982, to judge the islands themselves to be of at most marginal value to Britain, and still support the military action on the grounds that it is important to uphold the principle that international disputes should be resolved through peaceful means. This view need not be undermined by evidence of instances where Britain has appeared to turn a blind eye to comparable acts of aggression, because a friendly state was to blame or because declaratory opposition was not matched by strong action. If the principle of non-resort to force is believed to be important then it should not be ignored simply because governments do not follow it consistently. Sometimes governments may be outraged by the behaviour of another but may be unable to do much about it and therefore feel that the best course is to play down the indignant denunciations in order to ameliorate the effects. It so happened that in this case the British could do something about it. If it is accepted that the fault for giving the conflict a military dimension lay with Buenos Aires, then as a matter of principle it is hard to argue that London should simply have accepted the new situation, and it is important for international order that it did not.

What might be the objections to this position? The first might be that it accepts too easily the view that Argentina was the aggressor. UN Resolution 502 did not name Argentina as an aggressor. It did, however, clearly tilt in Britain's direction in that it required the withdrawal of Argentine forces from the Falklands before anything else could happen, including negotiations on the future status of the islands. It also required the British task force to turn round, but that could not be construed as an equality of obligation given the relative proximity of the two sets of forces to the contested territory.

From an Argentine perspective, it may have seemed that the British Government was using the incident over South Georgia as a pretext for the reinforcement of its military position in the South Atlantic. If this was believed, it was a misapprehension of British objectives at the time (although some in the Falkland Islands lobby argued that this should be the case). Such concern may have helped determine Argentina's decision to move while the military conditions were favourable. But explaining why Argentina acted the way it did is not to justify it – especially as the only reason to be concerned about British reinforcement was if it complicated a future attempt at occupation; Britain was not threatening Argentina itself.

There was great frustration in Buenos Aires over the failure to make progress on the issue of the Malvinas, a factor that again helps explain Argentine action without justifying it. There were other forms of pressure available to underline impatience. One obvious means would have been cutting off the sea and air links which Argentina supplied between the Falkland Islands and the mainland.

It is also the case that Argentina sought to occupy the islands with the minimum casualties, but this did not alter the fact that it was seizing territory by force. From statements made during the conflict there does seem to have been a widely held view among the international community that in so doing Argentina was violating an important international norm. Britain's Ambassador to the United Nations at the time, Sir Anthony Parsons, has testified to the importance of this principle in developing support for Britain, even among non-aligned countries which had hitherto generally supported Argentina on the question of sovereignty.

A second objection might be that international opprobrium, most notably in the form of economic sanctions, should have been used by Britain to force Argentina to leave the islands after the occupation. We do not know what would have happened if the British Government had decided *not* to send a task force. There are some indications that Argentina planned to remove its troops from the islands once it had succeeded in forcing the international community, especially the United States, to take note of this long-standing dispute. However, having taken the islands, the temptation to maintain the garrison might have proved irresistible. All the indications are that Argentine terms for a settlement hardened as a result of the occupation, at least initially, and that Argentina would have expected tangible results in the course of subsequent negotiations.

The international principle at stake could have been upheld without Britain responding by force of arms. In fact, Britain encouraged, successfully, the imposition of economic sanctions; but such sanctions are notoriously difficult to enforce, as there are always countries who feel under no obligation to respect them. Other Latin American countries could have helped break the sanctions. Moreover to some extent the exercise could have been counter-productive, not so much because of the loss of trade but because of the risk that Argentina would repudiate its substantial debts and create difficulties for the international financial system.

The most serious difficulty was that sanctions take time to work and in the waiting process the military option would have been lost for ever. In terms of both the climate and the potential improvements in the Argentine position, the Government either had to despatch the task force or acknowledge that there could be no resulting response, and once the task force was despatched it would have to be used within a few months before it would need to return home. The military option was available only for a limited duration; it could not be held in reserve.

As it was there was almost a month's diplomatic activity before the military confrontation began in earnest. Mediation was offered by the United States and accepted by both sides. This immediately raised the issue of to what extent the British Government was prepared to allow the Argentine Government to benefit as a result of its aggression. If it now got a better deal would not that reward aggression? Thus while there were marginal concessions on the conduct of the negotiations and the nature of an interim administration, Britain would not concede on the paramountcy of the islanders' wishes. Because the military confrontation had no predictable outcome, prior to the first battles neither side was under pressure to make concessions. Both sides criticized each other for a lack of seriousness in the negotiations but the underlying question was whether Argentina was to gain by an action that was in itself reprehensible. Because the confrontation itself would involve costs, there was incentive to find a diplomatic solution even if Argentina did obtain concessions. In the aftermath of the shocks of the *Belgrano* and the *Sheffield*, with the costs becoming all too apparent, Britain was for a while more conciliatory. Thus the principle that aggression must not be rewarded was less than absolute.

This brings us to the central question: what are these principles worth in blood and treasure? Before answering let us identify the costs. Some 1,000 people lost their lives. Injuries are hard to quantify but they certainly totalled thousands on both sides. The numbers scarred by the war, either through bereavement or the after-effects of combat are much greater still. For Britain at least the financial costs are easier to quantify – £780m on the campaign itself, £1,200m on protecting the islands against a recurrence throughout the rest of the 1980s. To this can be added extra civilian expenditure on the islands themselves to make them more economically viable. A third cost would be the breaking of diplomatic relations and the disruption of trade with a country with whom in all other respects there was good reason to be friendly.

Fourthly might be added a general estrangement with Latin America, although here matters become more complicated. Some Latin American countries were enthusiastic and genuine in their support for Argentina, for others it was more rhetorical and Chile was virtually in alliance with Britain. In practical terms the impact on Britain's relations with Latin America as a whole does not appear to have been great.

Fifthly we should consider the domestic political consequences, which to some might seem an added bonus but to others were a distinct cost. Some critics took exception to the nationalism, militarism, and eventually, triumphalism associated with a military campaign. This is an extraordinarily difficult charge to assess, in part because it is value-laden but also because it is by no means clear that the tendencies so deplored were either particularly widespread or have continued since.

Even concentrating on the most tangible costs we lack criteria against which to measure the benefits of the operation, or more accurately the costs of not responding by force. The islands themselves are not worth billions of pounds or a number of lives by any calculation. Presumably some compensation could have been arranged if they had been ceded to Argentina. Presumably too, Argentina would have been happy to have cooperated in setting up the islanders in some other equally congenial remote spot away from the South Atlantic, and this would have been at a fraction of the cost.

Putting a value on principles, however, is much more difficult. Take for example, the principle of self-determination. It is not an absolute but a matter of degree. In some areas if not in all, to some extent if not completely, some communities can shape their own destinies. It is generally agreed that foreign domination is the most serious challenge to self-determination. The islanders could have been settled somewhere else, possibly in greater comfort, but, if they wanted to stay in the Falklands and did not want to be ruled over by a foreign power through a military dictatorship with a poor record on human rights, what was it worth to liberate them? It was said that there were 'only 1,800' islanders, with the implication (often explicit) that their fate was not worth the loss of life and expenditure of resources. But at what point would their liberation have been important – if there had been 2,000, 4,000, 20,000, 100,000?

The same problem faces us with the principle that armed force should not be used to resolve international disputes. That Britain took a stand in this instance provides no guarantee that the principle will be taken more seriously elsewhere, but nor does this render the principle itself unimportant. Although it is the breaches that gain most attention, by and large this is a principle still more honoured in the observance than in the breach, and it is important for international order that this remains so. The value to be placed on this is in the end a matter of judgement.

Possible gains for Britain arising out of the campaign are also difficult to quantify. If the Argentine occupation had succeeded this would have been a blow to British prestige, and taken to confirm the end of Britain's era as a major power. Some might consider this a bonus on the grounds that such a role was already beyond Britain's resources and merely provided an excuse to retain the trappings of former imperial glories and to justify disproportionate expenditure on defence. (Britain devotes a significantly larger percentage of its GDP to defence than its European allies.) The number of countries now directly dependent upon Britain is small. Those that remain, were extremely supportive of the British operation – in Latin America, Belize relies on British protection against a Guatemalan threat and, to a far smaller extent, Guyana against Venezuela. Within Europe, Norwegians were impressed by the success of the British operation, largely because it employed units, equipment and techniques which have been designed for NATO's northern flank.

This discussion illustrates that there are no straightforward rules for deciding the question 'was it worth it?'. A cost–benefit analysis is made difficult by the fact that some of the alleged credits and debits are impossible to quantify, and that the view one takes of issues such as the importance of self-determination, or of not rewarding 'aggression', or of 'prestige', depends on one's own value system and broad understanding of international politics.

A final point is that this has been a retrospective judgement on the case for a military intervention, undertaken with the benefit of knowing its outcome. When the decision on intervention was taken, those responsible had reason to expect even greater casualties. On the other hand, they might have been more optimistic that a show of military strength would encourage Buenos Aires to back down without a fight. Those who opposed the sending of the task force (or its commitment to battle once it had arrived) did so because they were fearful that the human costs would be high and that the expedition would fail. If it had failed, or if the costs became intolerable (perhaps because of the loss of a carrier, or a troopship) such that the operation had to be called off before further disaster, then there would have been no doubt now that the whole enterprise was a ghastly mistake, that Britain should have accepted the humiliation of the Argentine success and then got the best terms available from Buenos Aires to settle the matter in as honourable way as possible under the circumstances. If the Argentine occupation had taken place a few months later when Britain lacked a serious military response then that would have been all the Government could have done. Our assessment is coloured by the fact that Operation Corporate succeeded.

A final point to conclude this section is that if the strongest part of the Government's case rests with the general principle of international behaviour rather than the specific question of the Falklands, then the question of the future of the islands remains open. If the argument is that it is wrong to solve disputes by force of arms, then the corollary is that it is equally important to demonstrate the possibility of disputes being solved by peaceful negotiations.

The Argentine occupation clearly changed the political situation in the South Atlantic, in that it made the islanders even more resistant to having much to do with the mainland and, as a result of the substantial British military and civilian investment, there was even less incentive to do so. On the other hand, the Argentine Junta was replaced by a democratic government in 1983. (It is arguable that the main beneficiaries of the war were the Argentine people in that failure in the war led directly to the fall of the Junta.) The logic that encouraged the Foreign Office to seek a negotiated settlement, perhaps in the form of a lease-back, still applies. It is not the case that because the blood of British soldiers was spilled over the Falklands the islands must now remain British forever. If that was a firm rule then Britain would still be a substantial imperial power. The need to respond in kind to the Argentine use of armed force was not a reflection of the strength of the British position in the Falklands.

The final set of questions concerns the conduct of the war. When a nation goes to war it must make calculations as to its likely course. The decision may be justified on the basis of calculations of expected cost which are over-optimistic or, as likely, over-pessimistic of the cost of *not* going to war. During the course of a campaign assessments of the various costs and benefits of its continuance alter. Thus some of the most important strategic decisions are taken *after* the initial commitment of forces and the consequences of these later decisions influence our views of the wisdom of the whole exercise. The die is not cast with the initial commitment. Rather the conflict is likely to proceed through distinct stages. This process has come to be known as 'escalation', although the word carries a connotation of violence of ever-increasing scope and intensity which may often be erroneous. As in the case of the Falklands, the most violent engagements may be early on (e.g. the *Belgrano*) while in the middle there may be a lull as forces re-group and are re-supplied. What happens is that the freedom of manoeuvre of the policy-makers at each stage narrows as a result of earlier decisions, and the choice becomes ever more closely dependent on the choices made by the opponent.

Thus at the start of April 1982 the despatch of the task force could be justified either as a means of reinforcing diplomacy or as an insurance policy to provide alternative options should diplomacy fail. When diplomacy was not yielding fruit, those who took the first position faced the difficult choice of either conceding the Argentine case, by withdrawing the task force, or accepting the need for stronger military measures as a means of further reinforcing the diplomatic effort. They could therefore support the re-taking of South Georgia on 25 April, especially as it did not involve substantial casualties. When this again failed to produce the necessary concessions, then the awkward choice recurred, and by this time the Argentine forces were more prepared for a confrontation, spurred on by the spectacle of the British task force steaming to the South Atlantic. By the start of May the diplomatic effort had faltered. While future military steps might then be justified in terms of forcing a diplomatic settlement, in practice they were going to be increasingly shaped by the need to obtain a decisive military solution to the problem. By June, with the successful landing at Port San Carlos and the battle of Goose Green behind them, British troops were advancing on Stanley. At this point the Argentine Junta was, not surprisingly, in a more conciliatory mood, but the British Government saw no need to make concessions because victory was in sight.

Appendix I
The Literature on the Conflict

I have some hopes of spending the last year of my university career in 2013 in the Public Record Office examining the newly released files on the Falkland Islands conflict of 1982, checking on the assessment of the conflict that I had made in the years immediately after it. There will undoubtedly be revelations in 2013, but there are less likely to be surprises. Moreover, whatever emerges from the files will require a knowledge of the instant histories of the 1980s if it is to be effectively interpreted.

The study of an international crisis is quite different from the study of foreign policy issues that develop over time. In both cases it is necessary to take account of the attitudes and behaviour of countries other than that under study, but with crises one of the most dominant features is the sheer tempo of events. This pressure of time has important consequences for historians. It means that the key decisions are not always taken in the constitutionally appropriate forum and the records are often hopelessly incomplete. The decision to change the rules of engagement which led to the sinking of the Argentine cruiser the *General Belgrano* was not taken by the full war cabinet. Nor was the preceding discussion, which was among a few relevant individuals rather than part of a formal meeting, minuted. In a crisis much business is done on the telephone, without anyone having the time to make notes of the call. Working drafts for key statements are not always kept. Even when historically minded people are doing their best amongst the chaos to preserve key material it is often extremely difficult to know at the time what will be considered important later.

For the historian of 2013 this will prove extremely frustrating: for the contemporary historian there are significant short-term compensations. With the stakes so high, any perceived mismanagement of the crisis comes in for intense scrutiny. Thus the initial failure to anticipate the strength of feeling in Argentina over this issue and to deter the occupation led to an Official Inquiry headed by Lord Franks.[1] Although the committee was cautious in the extreme in its major findings, the body of evidence provided in support is full and valuable, throwing light on those areas of the government machine concerned with intelligence assessment that can normally be only dimly perceived.

The Government was somewhat less forthcoming with the controversy resulting from the sinking of the *Belgrano*, the most costly engagement of the war in terms of human life. Because the initial rationale for the sinking – that the cruiser was closing in on the task force – was eventually revealed to be false, critics assumed that the true rationale was much more sinister. This led to excursions into the overall military situation and prospects for a diplomatic settlement (in particular, an initiative from the President of Peru). Although the most damaging allegations could not be sustained, the revelations resulting from the controversy (including those contained in evidence collected by the House of Commons Foreign Affairs Committee) are extremely helpful in making sense not only of this incident but of the overall diplomatic and military situation at this time.[2]

Another area that generated enormous interest was the Government's handling of the media during the crisis. This led to a full study by the Select Committee on Defence, whose hearings provided an opportunity for journalists and broadcasters to give voice to their frustrations immediately after the close of hostilities.[3] A study on Government–media relations (which had been sponsored by the Ministry of Defence) provides the fullest account of the workings of any part of the Government machine during the crisis.[4]

Because hard news of what was actually going on in Whitehall and in the South Atlantic was rather scarce while the conflict was under way, there was a huge appetite for attempts to tell the 'real' story. The fact that Britain won undoubtedly encouraged publishers to believe that there would be a healthy market for books on this subject. The most instant of the 'instant histories' was that put together by the Insight Team of the *Sunday Times*.[5] Like the others that were to follow, it was largely based on interviews with key participants at all levels. The problem with the dependence on memories in this way, coupled with the requirement of speedy publication, is not simply one of factual error, though that is a problem, but that the experiences have not been fully digested and the less obvious, but often critical, questions have yet to be asked. In this sense the slightly less instant history by Max Hastings and Simon Jenkins is much more successful and remains the best single account on the conflict, although new evidence does mean that a number of their judgements require a reappraisal.[6]

Otherwise the flow of information on the political side of the conflict has been disappointing, apart from that generated by the *Belgrano* controversy. Although three key members of the war cabinet left the Government over the next year – John Nott, Francis Pym and Cecil Parkinson – none has commented in detail on the affair, although Pym did give evidence to the Select Committee on Foreign Affairs. For the critical details we may have to wait until Margaret Thatcher writes her memoirs, (which on the current showing will be about the same time as the official records are released!). The relevant Parliamentary debates, which were extremely important in terms of the domestic politics of the conflict, have been gathered together in a useful form by HMSO. The researcher should note, however, that there has been for reasons of space a certain amount of attenuation and omission. Also they do not start until 2 April and so miss the important Commons session on 23 March on the South Georgia crisis.[7] On the American side, Alexander Haig has published his memoirs, which include a substantial amount on the Falklands. However, the fact that his book was published with a lengthy erratum slip indicates that his memory is not wholly reliable.[8]

By contrast with the political side there have been many military memoirs. The Government provided much of the raw information,[9] and this was supplemented by an authoritative account by the two key front-line commanders.[10] There have now been numerous accounts of the fighting, from the perspective of Falkland Islanders, army doctors and junior and senior officers.[11] More often than not they succeed in conveying the atmosphere of the conflict rather than helping explain the underlying military rationales for many of the actions taken. However, Brigadier (now General) Julian Thompson's memoir is very good in this regard, especially when one reads between the lines.[12] The first official history, by the Royal Navy's historian, has now been published, which further helps in sorting out the operational details.[13] Overall the material for understanding the course of the campaign at sea and on land is now excellent.[14]

The military material is important for an understanding of the political decision-making under way in London. Crisis management is distinguished by the interplay of diplomatic and military factors, mediated through the political system. Many of the problems with interpreting key events in the Falklands campaign have resulted from a failure to appreciate the operational factors weighing on the policy-makers as they assessed their options. The relationship between political direction and military implementation has proved to be a touchy subject in the public debate on the Falklands but it may actually contain some of the most important lessons for the future.

The related area where the full story is most cloudy is that of the actual negotiations. Britain's two senior diplomats in the United States – Sir Nicholas Henderson at the Washington embassy and Sir Anthony Parsons at the UN – have both published valuable accounts from their vantage points.[15] Although the accounts based on interviews with key political figures reveal a lot, we lack the authoritative material we have elsewhere. Here the records may help. As intriguing will be the general diplomatic effort, with for example, the EEC and Japan, and including such sensitive matters as collaboration with Chile.

As this survey is largely about the British side I have not included Argentine material. Readers wanting an insightful interpretation of the conflict from an Argentine perspective should read Virginia Gamba's analysis.[16] Professor Gamba and myself are currently collaborating on a detailed account of the interaction between the decision-making of the two sides which should be available in late 1988 or early 1989.

When the PRO open its 'Falklands files' there is something to look forward to. It will not be simply a question of comparing the new version of events with the old. The files will require a knowledge of the contemporary commentary to help interpret them. The impressions of what was going on, the relationship between the key personalities, are recorded in the instant histories in a way that even the surviving participants will be unable to recall in 2013.

Notes

1 Falkland Islands Review: Report of a Committee of Privy Counsellors, Chairman, the Rt Hon. the Lord Franks, Cmnd 8787 (London: HMSO, 1983).

2 *Events of the Weekend of 1st and 2nd May 1982*, Third Report of the Foreign Affairs Committee, Session 1984–5 (London: HMSO, 1985). The most substantial case against the Government, although now discredited in several respects, is found in Desmond Rice and Arthur Gavshon, *The Sinking of the Belgrano* (London: Secker and Warburg, 1984).

3 *Handling of Press and Public Information During the Falklands Conflict*, First Report of the House of Commons Defence Committee, Session 1982–3 (London: HMSO, 1982).

4 Derrick Mercer et al., *The Fog of War* (London: Heinemann, 1987). See also, Valerie Adams, *The Media and the Falklands Campaign* (London: Macmillan, 1986) which examines the role played by defence commentators and pundits and was also sponsored by MoD.

5 The Sunday Times Insight Team, *The Falklands War: the Full Story* (London: Sphere, 1982).

6 Max Hastings and Simon Jenkins, *The Battle for the Falklands* (London: Michael Joseph, 1983).

7 House of Commons, *The Falklands Campaign: a Digest of Debates in the House of Commons 2 April to 15 June 1982* (London: HMSO, 1982).

8 Alexander Haig, *Caveat* (London: Weidenfeld and Nicolson, 1984).

9 See Secretary of State for Defence, *The Falklands Campaign: the Lessons*, Cmnd 8758 (London: HMSO, 1982); Supplement to the *London Gazette*, Friday 8 October 1982.

10 Admiral J. Woodward and General J. Moore, 'The Falklands experience', *Journal of the Royal United Services Institute*, March 1983.

11 John Smith, *74 Days: an Islander's Diary of the Falklands Occupation* (London:

Century Publishing, 1984); Rick Jolly, *The Red and Green Life Machine: a Diary of the Falklands Field Hospital* (London: Century Publishing, 1983); Nick Vaux, *March to the South Atlantic* (London: Buchan and Enright, 1986). For a corrective to the reminiscences of survivors see the letters of David Tinker, killed on *HMS Glamorgan*, *A Message from the Falklands* (London: Junction Books, 1982).

12 Julian Thompson, *No Picnic* (London: Secker and Warburg, 1985).

13 David Brown, *The Royal Navy and the Falklands War* (London: Leo Cooper, 1987); Eric Grove's history of the post-war Royal Navy, *Vanguard to Trident: British Naval Policy Since World War Two* (Annapolis, Md; Naval Institute Press, 1987) contains valuable material on the Falklands.

14 See for example, Martin Middlebrook, *Operation Corporate: the Story of the Falklands War 1982* (London: Viking, 1985); Jeffrey Ethell and Alfred Price, *Air War South Atlantic* (London: Sidgwick and Jackson, 1983).

15 Sir Anthony Parsons, 'The Falklands crisis in the United Nations, 31 March–14 June 1982', *International Affairs*, Spring 1983; Sir Nicholas Henderson, 'America and the Falklands', *The Economist*, 12 November 1983.

16 Virginia Gamba, *The Falklands/Malvinas War: a Model for North–South Crisis Prevention*, (London: Allen and Unwin, 1987).

Appendix II
Opinion Polls Cited

MORI

The Economist *Panel*

  I 14 April 1982: 1,018 adults aged 18+ interviewed across
     53 constituency sampling points across Great Britain.
  II 20–21 April 1982: 463 of original respondents
     re-interviewed by telephone.
III 23–24 April 1982: 447 of original respondents
     re-interviewed by telephone. This poll was used by BBC
     Panorama.
IV 3–5 May 1982: 526 of original respondents
     re-interviewed, 113 face-to-face and 413 by telephone.
  V 25–26 May 1982: 400 of original respondents
     re-interviewed by telephone.
VI 21–23 June 1982: 501 of original respondents
     re-interviewed, 183 face-to-face and 318 by telephone.

Other MORI polls

  26 April 1982: 600 adults aged 18+ interviewed at 100 constituency sampling points throughout Great Britain for the *Daily Star*.

  30 April 1982: 1,178 adults aged 18+ interviewed across 53 constituency sampling points throughout Great Britain.

  The MORI poll evidence for April and May was discussed in Robert Worcester and Simon Jenkins, 'Britain rallies round the Prime Minister', *Public Opinion*, June/July 1982.

Gallup

The Gallup findings are taken from the Gallup Political Index nos 261 and 262.

National opinion polls

5 April, 942 adults in 47 constituencies.

Index